Barbarossa 1941

German Infantryman
VERSUS
Soviet Rifleman

COMBAT

David Campbell

First published in Great Britain in 2014 by Osprey Publishing,
PO Box 883, Oxford, OX1 9PL, UK
PO Box 3985, New York, NY 10185-3985, USA
E-mail: info@ospreypublishing.com

Osprey Publishing is part of the Osprey Group

© 2014 Osprey Publishing Ltd.

All rights reserved. Apart from any fair dealing for the purpose of private study, research, criticism or review, as permitted under the Copyright, Designs and Patents Act, 1988, no part of this publication may be reproduced, stored in a retrieval system, or transmitted in any form or by any means, electronic, electrical, chemical, mechanical, optical, photocopying, recording or otherwise, without the prior written permission of the copyright owner. Enquiries should be addressed to the Publishers.

A CIP catalogue record for this book is available from the British Library

Print ISBN: 978 1 4728 0324 5
PDF ebook ISBN: 978 1 4728 0325 2
ePub ebook ISBN: 978 1 4728 0326 9

Index by Alan Thatcher
Typeset in Univers, Sabon and Adobe Garamond Pro
Maps by bounford.com
Originated by PDQ Media, Bungay, UK
Printed in China through Asia Pacific Offset Ltd

14 15 16 17 18   10 9 8 7 6 5 4 3 2 1

Osprey Publishing is supporting the Woodland Trust, the UK's leading woodland conservation charity, by funding the dedication of trees.

www.ospreypublishing.com

Dedication
With thanks, to Mr Terry Braddock and Mr John Davies.

Acknowledgements
The author would like to thank: Geoff Banks; John Calvin, wwii-photos-maps.com; Graham Campbell; David Greentree; Dr Frank Price; Sheila Urbanoski; Marek Zielinski, Mapywig.org; and the staff of Southsea Library.

Author's note
All translations from sources published in German and Russian are the author's own.

Editor's note
While German-language terms are used for German ranks, Soviet ranks are translated into English. Soviet unit designations are given in English and in full, while German unit titles are given in their German-language form and are abbreviated at regimental level and below.

As the Germans and Soviets used the metric system of measurement in World War II, metric units of measurement are employed in this book.

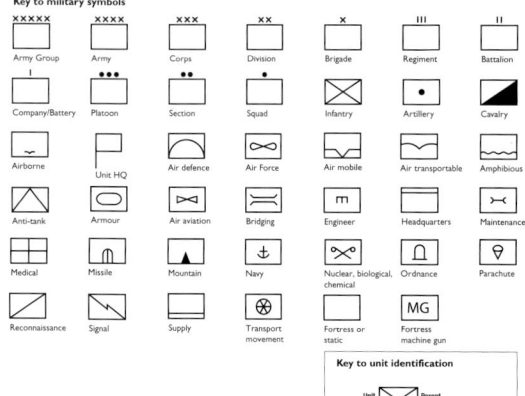

Comparative ranks

US Army, 1941	German	Soviet*
General of the Army	Generalfeldmarschall	Márshal Sovétskogo Soyúza (Marshal of the Soviet Union)
n/a	n/a	Generál ármii (General of the Army)
General	Generaloberst	Generál-Polkóvnik (Colonel-General)
Lieutenant-General	General	Generál-Leytenánt (Lieutenant-General)
Major-General	Generalleutnant	Generál-Mayór (General-Major)
Brigadier-General	Generalmajor	n/a
Colonel	Oberst	Polkóvnik (Colonel)
Lieutenant-Colonel	Oberstleutnant	Podpolkóvnik (Sub-Colonel)
Major	Major	Mayór (Major)
Captain	Hauptmann	Kapitán (Captain)
1st Lieutenant	Oberleutnant	Stárshiy Leytenánt (Senior Lieutenant)
n/a	n/a	Leytenánt (Lieutenant)
2nd Lieutenant	Leutnant	Mládshiy Leytenánt (Junior Lieutenant)
Sergeant-Major	Stabsfeldwebel	Starshiná (Sergeant-Major)
Master Sergeant	Oberfeldwebel	n/a
Technical Sergeant	Feldwebel	n/a
Staff Sergeant	Unterfeldwebel	Stárshiy Serzhánt (Senior Sergeant)
Sergeant	Unteroffizier	Serzhánt (Sergeant)
n/a	Stabsgefreiter	Mládshiy Serzhánt (Junior Sergeant)
Corporal	Obergefreiter	n/a
n/a	Gefreiter	Yefréytor (Lance-Corporal)
Private First Class	Oberschütze, Obersoldat	n/a
Private	Schütze, Soldat	Ryadovóy, Krasnoarmeyets (Private, Red Army man)

*Junior officers (Junior Lieutenant–Captain) in rifle divisions would have an accompanying political officer, a *Politruk*, and senior officers (up to army commanders) a commissar.

CONTENTS

INTRODUCTION	4
THE OPPOSING SIDES	9
Origins and combat role • Recruitment, morale and logistics • Leadership and communications • Armament, training and tactics	
ZHLOBIN	29
6 July 1941	
SMOLENSK	45
15–23 July 1941	
VAS'KOVO–VOROSHILOVO	57
23–27 July 1941	
ANALYSIS	72
Lessons learned: the Germans • Lessons learned: the Soviets	
AFTERMATH	76
UNIT ORGANIZATIONS	78
BIBLIOGRAPHY	79
INDEX	80

Introduction

'The whole thing should be over in three or four weeks, they said, others were more cautious and gave it two or three months. There was even one who said it would take a whole year, but we laughed him right out. "Why, how long did the Poles take us, and how long to settle France?"' (quoted in Kershaw 2010: 22). So said Schütze Benno Zeiser, recalling the bright confidence with which he and most of his comrades greeted the idea of invading the Soviet Union. Operation *Barbarossa*, launched at 0315hrs on Sunday 22 June 1941, was the largest invasion in the history of warfare in the midst of probably the most significant war in modern human experience. It was the defining act of the European theatre of war, setting the course of the conflict for the next four years in a struggle whose vast scope often disguises the reality of the conflict as much as it explains it.

For the ordinary German infantryman or Soviet rifleman, though, the enormity of such a stage was all but invisible, an abstraction for the most part that bore only a tangential relationship to the practical and immediate reality of movement, attack and defence. The success of one's army or nation was seen and understood through the prism of everyday experience, an experience that had been rather harsh for Soviet soldiers who had endured the relative failures of the Polish campaign and the outright embarrassments of Finland a few months later. However, to be a German soldier in the early summer of 1941 was quite something. The nation fielded a professional, experienced army, the Heer, with successful campaigns in Poland, Norway, France and the Low Countries, Yugoslavia and Greece, an army that had employed new armoured and combined-arms tactics to great strategic effect.

For the Germans, the prospective war in the East was from the very beginning ideological, its reasoning knotted together from policies like *Lebensraum* ('living space', the idea that 'superior' races would have the need and the right to expand into lands of 'inferior' races), virulent anti-communism, disgust at the perceived racial inferiority of the Slavic peoples, and an ideal of a pan-Germanic state that would stretch through East Prussia and Poland into Byelorussia and the Ukraine, uniting ethnic Germans across the East. For the men and women of the Soviet Union the rapacity of their Teutonic neighbours raised few qualms, however, protected as they felt they were behind the practical buffer of eastern Poland and the political buffer of 1939's Molotov–Ribbentrop Pact. That they were ideological enemies was never in doubt, and there was certainty that war would be inevitable at some stage, but it seemed unlikely that Hitler would open a new front while still fighting against Britain in the West, and while the German state still received so many vital goods (e.g. petroleum, chromium) from the Soviet Union in trade.

The decision to invade the Soviet Union was confirmed by Hitler's Directive 21 on 18 December 1940. The plan called for a massive invasion across the frontier; there were two thrusts, split by the Pripet Marshes. To the north, Heeresgruppe Nord would make for Leningrad and Heeresgruppe Mitte would attack towards Minsk, then Smolensk and ultimately Moscow, while to the south Heeresgruppe Süd would strike into the Ukraine towards Kiev. All three *Heeresgruppen* were tasked with the destruction of the Soviet Union's armed forces and the subsequent capture of economically and strategically valuable targets, with the majority of the Wehrmacht's might being concentrated in Generalfeldmarschall Fedor von Bock's Heeresgruppe Mitte, a force of 51 divisions that included two great armoured formations, Generaloberst Heinz Guderian's Panzergruppe 2 and Generaloberst Hermann Hoth's Panzergruppe 3.

Opposing the Germans was the Red Army, formally known as the RKKA (*Raboche-krest'yanskaya Krasnaya armiya*, or 'Workers' and Peasants' Red Army'). This vast force of over five million men – well over two million of whom were defending the western approaches of the Soviet Union – was equipped

OPPOSITE

German infantry catch an impromptu ride, sitting on the folded-down side panels of an SdKfz 10/4 mounting a 2cm FlaK 30/38 cannon. For the Wehrmacht, motorization was not just a matter of equipping infantry with trucks to allow them to move about more quickly. Using mobility, flexibility and the rapid concentration of force and firepower to achieve decisive results, the motorized-infantry regiments were an integral part of the complex and highly trained combined-arms teams that made the great tactical and operational successes of Blitzkrieg possible. In the first six weeks of the invasion the men of Infanterie-Regiment (mot.) 41, Infanterie-Regiment (mot.) 15 and Infanterie-Regiment (mot.) *Großdeutschland* would fight their way through three echelons of increasingly vicious and resistant Soviet armies. The three engagements featured in this book – an encounter battle, contesting a city and then clashing along a dangerously stretched perimeter – show the Germans' shift from offensive to defensive fighting, as well as the limitations of motorized-warfare tactics. (Nik Cornish at www.stavka.org.uk)

Central sector, Operation *Barbarossa*, June and July 1941

1 **22–27 June:** the Axis invasion begins at 0315hrs on 22 June; Generalfeldmarschall Fedor von Bock's Heeresgruppe Mitte – consisting of 4. Armee, 9. Armee, Generaloberst Hermann Hoth's Panzergruppe 3 and Generaloberst Heinz Guderian's Panzergruppe 2 – strikes across the Bug River, bypassing the fortress of Brest-Litovsk to the north and south. Bock's *Panzergruppen* lance forward in a giant pincer movement to envelop Bialystok and Minsk, snapping shut on 27 June.

2 **22 June–4 July:** 10. Infanterie-Division (mot.), commanded by Generalleutnant Friedrich-Wilhelm Löper, moves into Byelorussia with General der Panzertruppen Leo Geyr von Schweppenburg's XXIV. Armeekorps (mot.), which also includes 3. and 4. Panzer-Divisionen. 10. Infanterie-Division (mot.) moves along the Brest-Litovsk highway, helps to stem an attempted break-out from the Bialystok–Minsk *Kessel*, passes through Sluzk and arrives at Bobruisk on the Berezina River, crossing over on a pontoon bridge on 4 July.

3 **22 June–3 July:** 29. Infanterie-Division (mot.), commanded by Generalmajor Walter von Boltenstern, moves across the border to the north of Brest-Litovsk with General der Panzertruppe Joachim Lemelsen's XXXXVII. Armeekorps (mot.), which also includes 17. and 18. Panzer-Divisionen. The division moves up 'R2' (Rollbahn 2 – the main Warsaw–Minsk highway), helps in the fighting around the edges of the Minsk *Kessel*, and strikes east towards the Dnieper River.

4 **27 June–2 July:** Infanterie-Regiment (mot.) *Großdeutschland* – a part of General der Panzertruppe Heinrich von Vietinghoff's XXXXVI. Armeekorps (mot.), together with 10. Panzer-Division and SS-Division *Reich* – finally crosses the Bug; the lavishly equipped reinforced regiment heads for the southern edge of the rapidly developing Bialystok–Slonim *Kessel*.

5 **4–6 July:** 10. Infanterie-Division (mot.) moves out from Bobruisk to the south-east, its orders to clear troops from the southern flank of XXIV. Armeekorps (mot.) and seize the river crossing at Zhlobin. The division runs straight into the advancing Soviet battle group led by Colonel Spyridon S. Chernyugov; the Soviets are forced back across the river with heavy losses, but they destroy the bridges at Zhlobin as they go.

6 **10–11 July:** Panzergruppe 2 forces its way across the Dnieper to the north and south of the Soviet stronghold of Mogilev, with 29. Infanterie-Division (mot.) at Kopys, *Großdeutschland* at Shklov and 10. Infanterie-Division (mot.) at Bykhov.

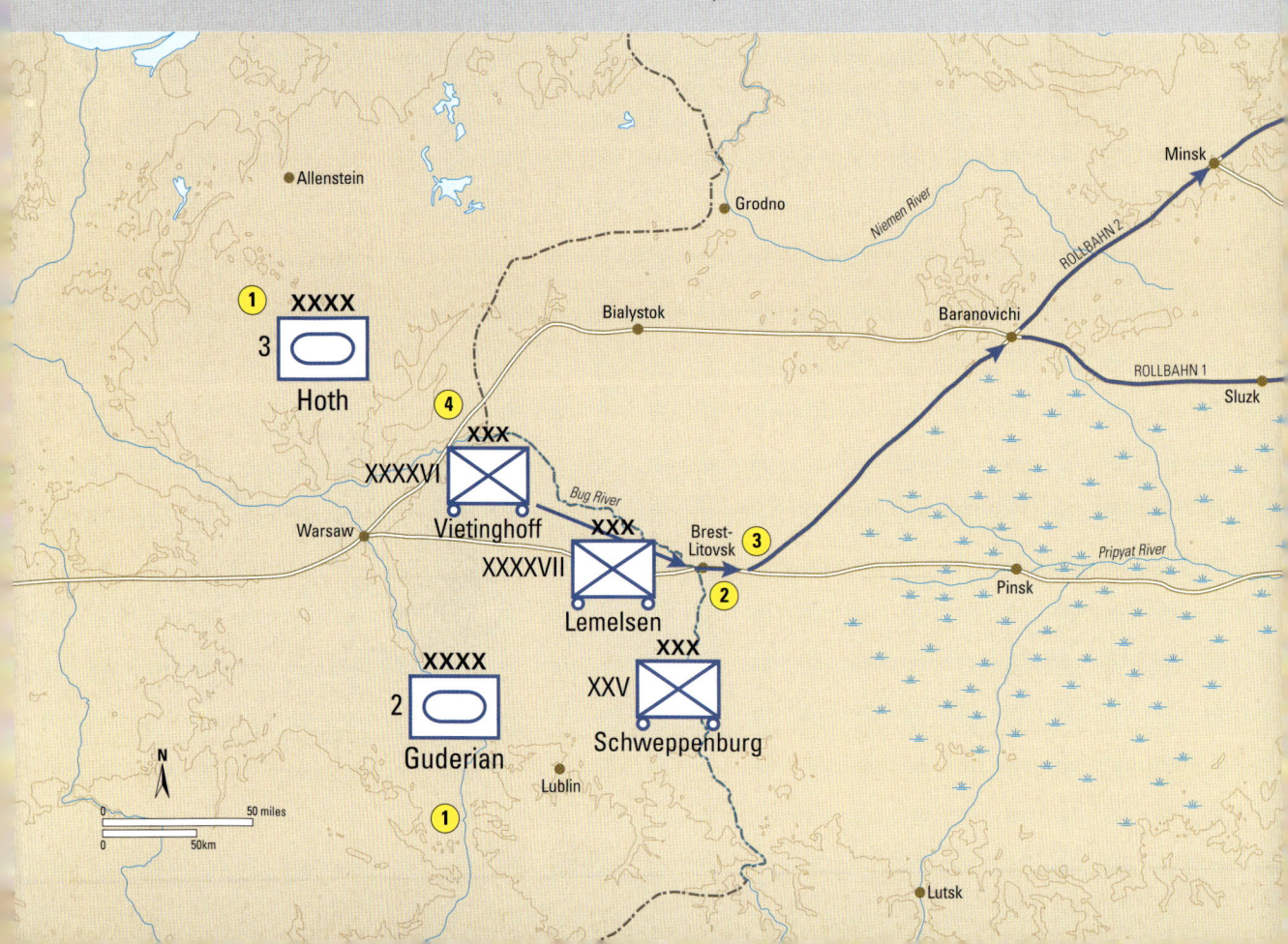

7 **15–23 July:** 29. Infanterie-Division (mot.) penetrates the southern half of Smolensk on 15 July and on the following day storms across the Dnieper to wrest the northern half of the city from Lieutenant-General Mikhail F. Lukin's 16th Army. This German success is immediately challenged by Soviet counter-attacks that pin 29. Infanterie-Division (mot.) in the city, forcing it to fight a vicious and costly urban battle.

8 **17–21 July:** *Großdeutschland* moves out from Gorky, its job to keep open the advance road of 10. Panzer-Division (which has been fighting further ahead), as well as to guard the Propoisk–Roslavl road on Panzergruppe 2's southern flank. The regiment moves into defensive positions around the villages of Vas'kovo and Voroshilovo.

9 **23–27 July:** Using four newly created armies, Marshal of the Soviet Union Semyon K. Timoshenko launches a huge counter-strike against the German forces that are surrounding Smolensk; regiments from 145th and 149th Rifle divisions (part of Lieutenant-General Vladimir Y. Kachalov's 28th Army) begin a series of unceasing attacks against *Großdeutschland*'s positions that set the tone for much of the coming month's fighting. The battle of Smolensk ends in defeat for the RKKA, but for the Wehrmacht, especially the motorized formations, the victory is a Pyrrhic one.

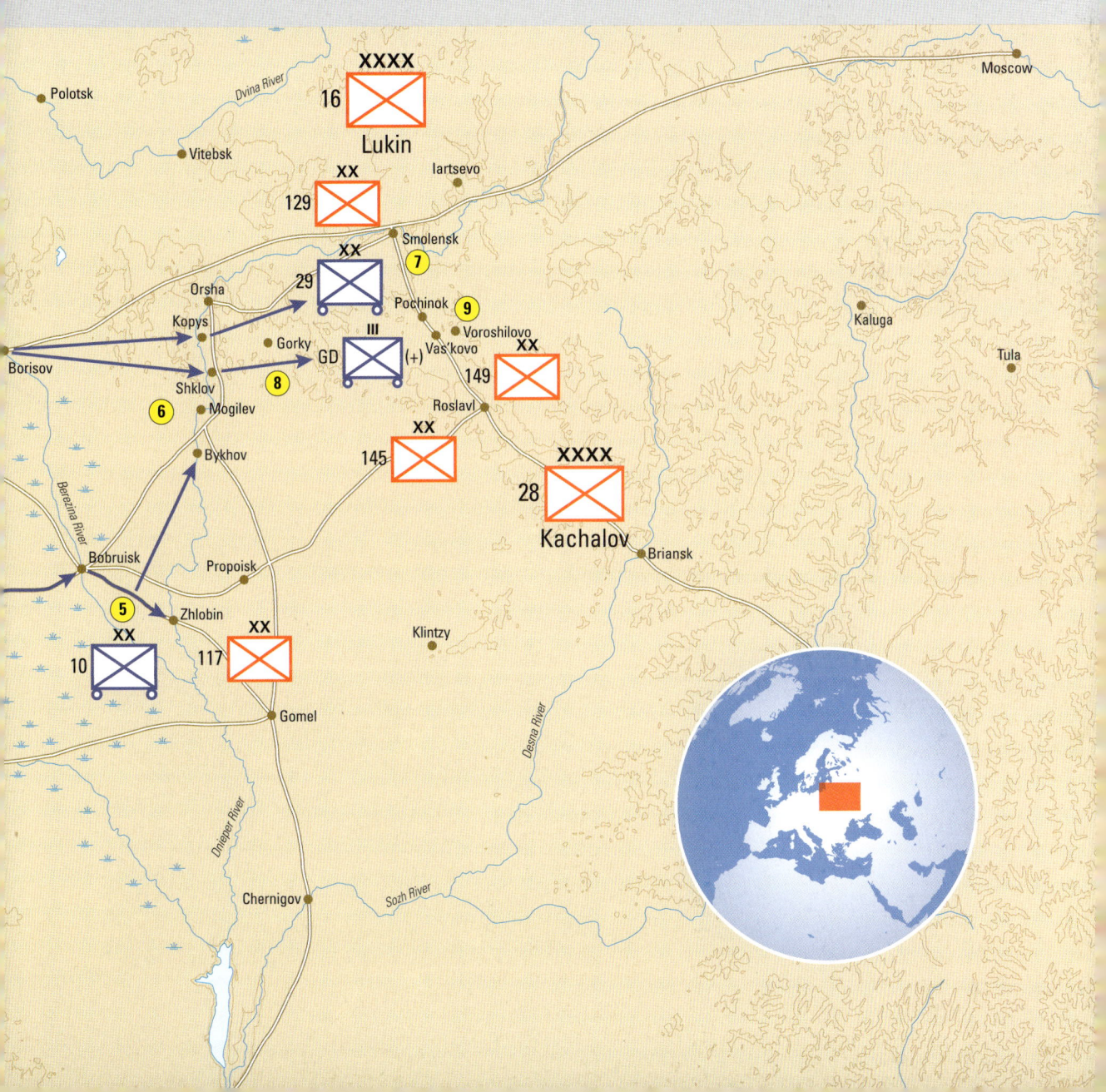

Red Army infantry advance across the open steppe, with some soldiers taking advantage of a lift on the back of a passing T-34. Despite lacking the superficial glamour of that organization's mechanized forces or the raw power of its artillery, the ordinary riflemen of the RKKA – under-equipped, over-stretched and in most cases tactically over-matched – would make the difference in checking the fast-moving maelstrom of the German advance. Their aggression and reliance on the attack, their stubbornness in defeat, and their willingness to spend lives on a scale that was almost incomprehensible to their opponents, would, by the end of July, confirm for the more astute German observers that the war they were fighting now wasn't the one they started six short weeks earlier. The men who made up these rifle regiments were not rabid Communists hobbled by ideology or semi-savage Slavs incapable of coherent action, as some of their German enemies thought; they were, as all national armies are, a reflection of the breadth and complexities of their homeland, a homeland that the Wehrmacht both underestimated and misunderstood. (From the fonds of the RGAKFD in Krasnogorsk via Stavka)

with reliable weapons, significant mechanized forces (including many modern tanks) and excellent artillery in copious quantities. Even with the benefit of surprise, the German forces would expect to be hard pressed in a fight with such a large and dangerous foe, and yet their plans called for the destruction of all western Soviet armies within six weeks, followed by a series of strategic advances that would take the invaders all the way to the Ural Mountains. Such ambition would seem extraordinarily hubristic if taken without regard to the almost miraculous-seeming series of victories that had brought the Germans to this point.

For Heeresgruppe Mitte the advance on Smolensk was the first strategic objective. The Panzer and motorized-infantry divisions of Guderian's and Hoth's *Panzergruppen* were the key – they had the speed, the flexibility and the striking power to drive deep into the Soviet defences, bypassing strongpoints and wrong-footing the Border armies. The first six weeks of the campaign would see Heeresgruppe Mitte do just that, but would also show the serious, potentially devastating miscalculations that the Wehrmacht had made about the capabilities of their own forces as well as those of their enemy.

The Heer's standard divisional light howitzer, a 10.5cm leFH 18 (*leichte Feldhaubitze*, or 'light field howitzer 18') struggles with its limber up a rough Russian slope. For motorized-infantry formations, however, the job of hauling the gun was done by prime movers such as the half-tracked SdKfz 251/4. (Nik Cornish at www.stavka.org.uk)

The Opposing Sides

ORIGINS AND COMBAT ROLE

German

Generaloberst Hans von Seeckt, commander of Germany's Reichsheer in the wake of World War I, planned to build a force that – massively expanded – would fight in any new conflicts with the understanding and expectation that '"tactics depend upon co-operation between arms" and that the next war would be one of "Manoeuvre"' (quoted in Westwood 2002: 05). Drawing upon a German tradition of reliance upon speed and overwhelming force to bring the enemy to a decisive, annihilating battle, Seeckt encouraged the development of mobile tactics and weapons systems and an innovative approach to armoured warfare. This was taken far further than he had

A group of motorized *Feldgendarmerie* at rest beside their truck, most probably a Citroën T23 – note the MG 34 on an AA mount. Motorization was a comprehensive process covering every aspect of the division. In comparison a regular infantry division would be reliant upon horsepower, its only significant motorized components being the anti-tank and reconnaissance battalions. All sorts of 2- to 3-tonne vehicles were used for troop transport, most notably the petrol-engine Opel Blitz, but also the diesel-engine Daimler-Benz L3000 A and S models, plus trucks from Ford, Citroën and other manufacturers (through purchase or capture). The trucks gave motorized divisions their mobility, but they were of limited use off-road, and even on-road they suffered excessive wear and tear due to the rough and ready conditions of Soviet infrastructure. (Nik Cornish at www.stavka.org.uk)

envisaged by men like Major (later Generaloberst) Heinz Guderian and Generalleutnant Oswald Lutz, the chief of the new *Panzertruppe* branch from 1934. The development of the *Panzertruppe* nurtured an appreciation of combined-arms operations, and there was an understanding that the new Panzer divisions, despite each possessing an integral complement of infantry – the *Schützen-Regimenter* ('rifle regiments') – would benefit from the support of equally mobile dedicated units to supplement and further exploit the expected victories of those divisions.

To this end four infantry divisions (2., 13., 20. and 29.) were motorized in October 1937 and fought in Poland and the West in 1939–40. During the build-up to the invasion of the Soviet Union the number of Panzer divisions was doubled, which stretched the available supply of Panzers to the limit and necessitated an increase in motorized units as well. The allocation of infantry to the Panzer divisions (at this time usually 2–4 battalions per division) was deemed sufficient for the immediate support of Panzer operations, but not for the broad, manpower-heavy requirements that arose during deep penetrations or large envelopments; here the motorized infantry, able to keep pace and interact with the Panzers, would prove invaluable. A further eight infantry divisions – 3., 10., 14., 16., 18., 25., 36. and 60. – were motorized by the end of 1940, with two – 16. and 60. – being deployed to the Balkans in the first half of 1941. Two of the four existing motorized divisions, 2. and 13. Infanterie-Divisionen (mot.), had been converted into Panzer divisions by June 1941, leaving ten motorized divisions, plus Infanterie-Regiment (mot.) *Großdeutschland*, available to take the field in the opening stages of *Barbarossa*.

Initially the motorized divisions had been comparable in strength to their footslogging counterparts (each of which averaged 17,734 all ranks), but they had proved to be somewhat unwieldy in 1939 so by the end of 1940's motorization programme each division had lost its third infantry regiment, leaving such formations with an establishment of 14,319 all ranks each by June 1941. The number of motorized-infantry regiments in these divisions increased from 12 in 1939 to 20 in mid-1941; of the original 12, however, only five retained the same designation, while the other seven had been converted into *Schützen* and/or *Kradschützen* serving within recently formed Panzer divisions. Infanterie-Regiment (mot.) *Großdeutschland* was expanded after the French campaign, leaving it a reinforced regiment of 20 companies (in five battalions) with an attached artillery battalion (ArtAbt 400), over 6,000 men strong. There were also four SS motorized-infantry divisions included in *Barbarossa*, identical in structure to their Heer counterparts (with the exception of *Leibstandarte-SS Adolf Hitler*, which, although technically a division, was still only at brigade-strength): SS-Infanterie-Division (mot.) *Reich* in Panzergruppe 2, SS-Totenkopf-Division (mot.) in Panzergruppe 4, and SS-Division (mot.) *Wiking* and SS-Division (mot.) *Leibstandarte-SS Adolf Hitler* in Panzergruppe 1.

Soviet

Formed by Leon Trotsky in June 1918 to meet the immediate security needs of the new Bolshevik state, the RKKA came to reflect the society that spawned it, a place of opportunity for some and dreary servitude for others, an organization weighed down by dogma and shot through with fear. The 1920s and 1930s were times of experimentation and often radical thought about weapons and warfare, and 'if there was one army in the world that was obsessed with the possibilities of tanks, aircraft, and airborne, it was the Red Army' (Citino 2011: 127). Notable not just for its innovation in the theory and practice of airborne forces, the RKKA had been developing a large mechanized arm that was supposed to consist of 29 mechanized corps by mid-1942, though the arrival of the war found this force only half-built. Lacking structural flexibility and doctrinal sharpness, these corps were in no way comparable to the Germans' motorized corps or the Panzer divisions.

Conversely, the rifle divisions accounted for 75 per cent of the RKKA's strength, and were the Soviet Union's most significant asset in attack or defence. A rifle division in April 1941 ideally consisted of 'three rifle regiments of three battalions each plus two artillery regiments (one gun and one howitzer), a light tank battalion, and supporting services' (Glantz 2010: 27),

From around 855,000 men in 1934 the RKKA had grown to more than 1.3 million by 1939 (Merridale 2005: 52), with millions more in reserve. It had modern weapons, huge numbers of tanks and artillery, and, on paper at least, was the world's most formidable force. All was not well, however. The RKKA underwent three major reorganizations in the two years prior to the invasion (September 1939, June 1940 and April 1941) in an attempt to 'expand, reorganize, reequip, and reform its Armed Forces' (Glantz 2010: 26). In addition 'It was attempting to implement a defensive strategy with operational concepts based on the offensive deep battle (*glubokii boi*) and the deep operations (*glubokaia operatsiia*) theory developed in the 1930s to the detriment of effective defense at the operational (army) level' (Glantz 2010: 26). Here, RKKA infantry advance across open ground through a battery of mortars (either 82mm BM-37 or 120mm M1938 models) with the support of direct artillery fire, supplied by a 76mm divisional gun M1939 (USV). (Nik Cornish at www.stavka.org.uk)

At the start of the war the RKKA's artillery was its most effective, and dangerous, arm. With more than 67,000 guns and howitzers in June 1941, the Soviet artillery was well equipped and its crews were generally well trained, but the problems of unwieldy command structures and undermanning that affected other arms were also issues here, as were basic practical considerations like the efficient and regular supply of ammunition. Medium pieces like the 152mm M1937 (ML-20) howitzer-gun shown here were each crewed by nine men (one NCO and eight enlisted men), firing a substantial 44kg shell that could outrange its German counterpart (the 15cm sFH 18) by several thousand metres. Each rifle corps had two regiments of guns; these were either howitzer regiments (each with 36 152mm guns) or mixed regiments (each with 12 152mm and 24 107mm or 122mm guns), resources permitting. Such weapons could also be found in the army-level artillery regiments of the RGVK (*Rezerv Verkhovnogo Glavnokomandovaniya*, or 'Reserve of the Supreme Command'). (Courtesy of the Central Museum of the Armed Forces, Moscow via Stavka)

but the reality was more stark: the tanks rarely appeared, and though the authorized strength was 14,483 men most divisions could only field 8,000–10,000. The rifle divisions were grouped in pairs or threes into rifle corps that had 'very little organic logistical support' (Glantz 1997: 17), which were in turn grouped into armies, each of which fielded three rifle corps, one mechanized corps, two or three artillery regiments and an anti-tank artillery brigade. The mechanized corps were often seen as supporting assets for the attacks of rifle divisions, a large-scale version of the old idea that the role of the tank is to support the advance of the infantryman, while the rifle divisions were entirely dependent on the railways and their own feet for mobility. Their failings were starkly apparent in the first weeks of the invasion; emergency measures would be taken, with rifle corps effectively abolished on 15 July 1941 and rifle divisions streamlined to take account of the realities of war (from 18,841 men in an M39 rifle division, to 14,483 men in an April M41 rifle division, down to 10,859 men in the emergency revised M41 rifle division, introduced from 24 July 1941).

The parent units of the regiments featured in this book – 117th, 129th and 145th Rifle divisions – differed very little from one another. All had the same organization; only 145th Rifle Division had seen any sort of action – in the closing stages of the Polish campaign – but by 1941 all three were in the same boat, lacking men, equipment, proper training, and experienced officers. The 1939 version of the rifle division was, on paper, comparable with its German infantry counterpart both in manpower and armament, despite the fact that 'the entire Red Army's logistical state in 1939, in terms of communications equipment, weaponry, maintenance, and fuel and ammunition supply was poor' (Glantz 1997: 14–15). Following the April 1941 changes a rifle division had nine infantry battalions to a German motorized-infantry division's six and five artillery battalions to the German three, as well as comparable divisional assets and a light-tank battalion for good measure. Both should have similar establishments –14,483 for the rifle division as opposed to 14,319 for the motorized-infantry division – but the reality didn't come close.

RECRUITMENT, MORALE AND LOGISTICS

German

Schütze Benno Zeiser joined the Heer in May 1941: 'Those were the days of fanfare parades, and "special announcements" of one "glorious victory" after another, and it was "the thing" to volunteer. It had become a kind of super holiday.

At the same time we felt very proud of ourselves and very important' (quoted in Kershaw 2010: 29). Zeiser's enthusiasm was muted somewhat after he started to encounter some of the wounded coming back from the front, one of whom gave him a more realistic impression of the campaign: '… it was pretty grim. The Reds were fighting desperately and we had had heavy losses. All the same, the advance was continuing swiftly, but it was at a price which made it clear we could not tell how long it would all be as, apart from anything else, the Russians had more men than we, many more' (quoted in Kershaw 2010: 290).

The cornerstone of Heer recruitment was the *Wehrkreis* (military district), each of which was responsible for the recruitment, training, supply and administration of troops. Infantry recruits faced a hard but effective 16-week basic training course, including some combined-arms training (usually using captured French or Czech tanks). This was followed by further training in the newly passed-out recruit's company, and later battalion, as he mastered the more particular practical skills of combined-arms combat and, in the case of motorized regiments, the procedures of mobile warfare.

At the start of *Barbarossa*, morale was high; the motorized divisions had given a good account of themselves in Poland and France, as well as the recent Balkan invasions, and they certainly shared some of the glamour of the Panzer divisions in being a major part of the new German way of war. Unit cohesion was strong; officers at battalion and regimental level were familiar faces, and the NCOs were a core of stability and continuity, neither group having been too seriously reduced in the war's earlier campaigns. Even so, being a member of a motorized-infantry unit put one at the forefront of the Wehrmacht's attacking forces, a fact that didn't escape the notice of SS-Hauptsturmführer Klinter of the motorized SS-Totenkopf-Division: 'Motorized transport is only there to make certain we poor Panzergrenadiers [the term used from mid-1942 onwards] are brought up against the enemy more often than our fellows in the infantry divisions. Before and after battle we always have to march just as far and of course fight, so that we have the dubious advantage of being in action more often' (quoted in Kershaw 2010: 224).

An SdKfz 231 8-rad *schwerer Panzerspähwagen* ('8-wheeled heavy armoured car') of a Panzer or motorized *Aufklärungs-Abteilung*, armed with a 2cm KwK 30/38 autocannon and co-axial MG 34, fords a river, sporting an officer with a flair for the dramatic. Unlike its sister the SdKfz 232, the SdKfz 231 lacked a radio, but both were reasonably effective vehicles with armour to protect against 7.92mm armour-piercing ammunition and had a range of 300km on the road (170km cross-country), though they were to prove rather vulnerable to the mud of the coming *Rasputitsa* (literally the 'time without roads'), where heavy spring and autumn rains would turn the landscape of the Steppe into a trackless quagmire. (Nik Cornish at www.stavka.org.uk)

The experience of those campaigns had refined how the motorized divisions organized themselves into combat groups, also providing much highly useful practice in the complex everyday necessities that were needed to keep their formations mobile and effective, as well as the logistics of supply (a critical factor for units so dependent on fuel) under real wartime conditions. The motorized divisions that reached their staging areas near the Bug River were well equipped. The general quality and level of equipment was good, but the rush to expand the motorized capability meant that many captured vehicles from the French, Polish and Czech campaigns were pressed into service, causing problems with spare parts and interoperability. Though both personal and heavy weapons were of a high quality the most common anti-tank gun, the PaK 36 (somewhat derisively known as the 'door knocker'), was even at the outset of the campaign known to be underpowered – and this before the shock encounters with T-34s and the KV tanks. That this new theatre would throw up radical new challenges from the very first day was not properly anticipated; the inadequacy of the maps, the unusually harsh roads, the extremes of weather and the ever-extending supply lines would all contribute to the punishing nature of the campaign. The 'wartime conditions' of *Barbarossa* were of a different order to those that they had experienced before.

Soviet

According to Colonel (later Marshal of the Soviet Union) Nikolai I. Krylov, 'The Russian soldier loves a fight and scorns death. He was given the order: "if you are wounded, pretend to be dead; wait until the Germans come up; then select one of them and kill him! Kill him with gun, bayonet, or knife. Tear his throat with your teeth. Do not die without leaving behind you a German corpse"' (quoted in Clark 1985: 43). Such bloodthirsty exhortations were a part of the narrative of RKKA life, where the language of command, training and education was entirely subsumed into the political vernacular of the state. In such an environment duty was to the Party, the state and the *Rodina* (Motherland), in that order; regimental or divisional pride, such a marked characteristic of German and other armies of the time, was discouraged.

New state organizations such as the Komsomol (*Kommunisticheskii Soyuz Molodyozhi*, or 'Young Communist's League') – a political organization where 'good citizenship' was instilled through ideological education as well as basic military practices like orienteering, marching and camping – provided the Soviet Union with a generation of potential artillerists, engineers, aviators, officers and commissars for the armed forces, including the RKKA, RKKF (Navy), VVS (Air Force) and PVO (Air Defence Force). Officers were drawn from a far broader section of society than in Tsarist times; the best candidates were creamed off for the NKVD (*Narodnyy Komissariat Vnutrennikh Del*, or 'People's Commissariat for Internal Affairs'), the VVS and the RKKA's engineer and artillery branches, with the infantry, as is often the case, at the back of the line. For the enlisted men, conscription came at 19 years old, and fed them into an army that was drawn mostly (around 80 per cent) from the peasant villages rather than the cities, men who came from a multitude of

Soviet infantrymen and artillerymen from the early period of the war showing admirable inter-unit bonhomie. Note the collar patches and insignia; the officer reading the letter is a major of infantry (two enamel bars for rank, the crossed rifles over a target indicating his branch of service), with a captain of artillery to his right (one enamel bar for rank, the crossed cannons showing his branch of service) and a senior sergeant of artillery (three enamel triangles and crossed cannons) to his left. When serving in the front line officers were often easy enough to distinguish from their men as they didn't carry the long Mosin-Nagant rifle (they were usually only armed with a pistol) or wear the otherwise ubiquitous greatcoat roll over their shoulders. Some officers also rode into battle to encourage their men (there was a notable example in the desperate defence of Minsk), though, as might be imagined, they tended not to last long when doing so. The *pilotka* cap, worn by all in this picture, was popular with officers and men both at rest and in the line, though regulations stipulated (with underwhelming levels of success) that when in combat the soldiers must wear helmets. (From the fonds of the RGAKFD in Krasnogorsk via Stavka)

ethnic backgrounds and who spoke in mutually unintelligible dialects or languages. The expansion of the 1930s wasn't accompanied by an equally large growth in infrastructure or planning, and the RKKA rifleman of 1939 would often find himself with shoddy or missing equipment, living in dismal accommodations and eating poor food, subjected to daily lectures on the importance of the Party, and more used to being employed on ad hoc agricultural projects than as a soldier.

Though a largely conscript army the fierceness with which the personnel of the RKKA fought the invaders from the very first was a cause for comment and (for the Germans) concern. Although the German high command, blinded to a degree by its own peculiar political ideology, believed that the RKKA was poorly led and filled with degenerate Slavs who had been weakened morally and intellectually by their sufferance under Bolshevism, the men of the RKKA were

> average Soviet citizens [who] fought for the USSR for several basic reasons: loyalty to the idea of historic Russia; normal obedience to the state; the fact that the USSR had been invaded, making it a 'just war'; the realisation that life would not be any better under Nazi German rule; because the war represented a great societal and historical task for the first post-revolution generation; and out of self-interest, hoping to improve their place in society through wartime service. (Reese 2011: 10)

The positive sense of defending one's homeland against a monstrous aggressor would not be fully adopted by the Stavka or the state until 1942. In the interim, endless exhortations to do one's duty were compounded with savage discipline and punishment for those who seemed unwilling to give all they had for the state. Executions of men at the very highest level, such as General of the Army Dmitry G. Pavlov, were matched in a more rudimentary way throughout the RKKA; NKVD patrols hunted for 'deserters' among the detritus of shattered divisions, and officers at all levels could avail themselves of on-the-spot shootings if they felt them appropriate.

Structurally speaking, the RKKA, barely capable of supporting itself in peacetime, was disastrously unprepared for a conflict on the scale of *Barbarossa*.

Generaloberst Heinz Guderian. A pugnacious and sometimes difficult officer, his ideas (developed in large part from his observations and experience as a signals officer in World War I, compounded with the theories of Britain's Captain Basil Liddell-Hart and especially Colonel J.F.C. Fuller) developed into a cohesive theory through a series of lectures and journal articles he produced throughout the 1920s while at the Inspectorate of Transport Troops. One of his early observations on the Anglo-French tank actions leading up to Berry-au-Bac in 1917 – that 'We can only conclude that the main striking force of an offensive resides in tanks, and it is a question of developing the other arms in such a way that they can keep up with them' (Guderian 2002: 67) – is an excellent example of how he saw the need not just to refocus the Heer, but to change it fundamentally. *Barbarossa* would show his brilliance in command, his intolerance for his superiors, his wilfulness and almost downright disobedience in pursuit of what he considered the correct strategic goals of the campaign, and his frustration that the rest of the field armies seemed unable, intellectually and practically, to keep up with him. (Nik Cornish at www.stavka.org.uk)

The existing supply structure was complex, sluggish and corrupt; it failed at almost every level from the supply of bullets and boots through to tanks and train cars, leaving the RKKA's rifle divisions short of vital support weapons and ammunition. Vehicles, when they were available, suffered from constant shortages of fuel, and when they broke down – which they often did due to poor maintenance and hard use – had to be abandoned as there were no spare parts with which to fix them.

LEADERSHIP AND COMMUNICATIONS

German

Drawing upon the experiences of World War I, the Heer afforded its junior officers and NCOs the initiative to re-interpret or discard their orders if the tactical situation demanded it. Though there was still room for *Befehlstaktik* (detailed orders), it was more common for commanders at every level to use *Auftragstaktik* (task-oriented orders). *Auftragstaktik* relied upon '"the independence of the lower commander" (*Selbständigkeit der Unterführer*). A commander's ability to size up a situation and act on his own was an equalizer for a numerically weaker army, allowing it to grasp opportunities that might be lost if it had to wait for reports and orders to climb up and down the chain of command' (Citino 2011: 128). This approach allowed relatively junior officers and NCOs to develop a great deal of practical experience, giving German units a deep capacity to absorb losses in officers and yet still retain their tactical capability (seen to some degree in the men of Infanterie-Regiment (mot.) *Großdeutschland*, who maintained a coherent defence at Vas'kovo–Voroshilovo despite serious losses under constant enemy attack).

The German field manuals of Dr Reibert (*Der Dienstunterricht im Heere*, or 'Service Instruction in the Army') and in particular the manual of leadership, *Truppenführung* ('troop leading'), gave officers a comprehensive set of rules for most combat situations. They stressed the need for an officer to be near the fighting to allow him both to understand the tactical situation and to make his will felt, and urged him never to forget that 'the first demand in war is decisive action' (Reichswehr 1933: 5). These principles, combined with the general aggressiveness with which German soldiers were taught to prosecute attacks and defences, and the energetic possibilities inherent in a fully motorized force, ensured that that the commanders of motorized-infantry regiments used their speed and flexibility to maximum effect.

German divisional communications benefited from well-made, reliable telephones and radio sets. Radio nets were invaluable for the command and control of Panzer and motorized forces, who relied upon good communications and strong forward leadership to understand the battlespace and mount effective, co-ordinated attacks. However, mobile infantry vehicles, with the exception of command vehicles, were not routinely equipped with radio sets, and the motorized-infantry regiments were equipped in much the same way as their foot-slogging comrades, four radios to a regiment, with four more for each battalion. There was usually a premium on speed for the despatch of orders, and it was the practice at battalion level or below to give sharp, direct orders orally; this tended to work in part due to the consistency of training at all levels, but also because *Auftragstaktik* orders tended not to need caveats or lots of ancillary detail.

Effective radio communications allowed motorized formations to make the most of their mobility in developing or unexpected situations, letting commanders develop *Schwerpunkt* ('point of maximum effort') attacks that exploited an enemy's localized weaknesses. Flank attacks and the use of the pincer movement (*Zangenbewegung*), sweeping double-envelopments, were also expected to be one of the primary tactical as well as strategic methods of attack, with the practised mobility of motorized *Kampfgruppen* ('battle groups') providing opportunities that non-motorized German infantry would be too slow to exploit, or to which the enemy's infantry would be too sluggish to respond. Frontal assaults, deemed to be costly, were discouraged.

Motorized infantry were expected to operate in close conjunction with a whole range of units, especially tanks, in a variety of circumstances. Terrain was a critical factor because – in addition to all the usual such issues facing troops in attack or defence – motorized forces had to rely upon road networks or favourable ground to make the most of their movement capabilities, owing to most wheeled vehicles' speed and manoeuvrability dropping dramatically once they were off the road. Villages, woods and other terrain that limited mobility and gave the enemy opportunities to make mischief had to be avoided if possible, and all officers in motorized formations were expected to give a great deal of attention to maps and aerial-reconnaissance imagery before launching their attacks (though the maps provided on the eve of the invasion proved to be of little use). Leutnant Horst Zobel, an officer of 3. Panzer-Division who served through *Barbarossa*, summed up the four principles involved in leading motorized troops:

> (1) Motorized, especially armoured troops, have to be led from a position well forward. (2) Leading on the battlefield has to be carried out by short orders, primarily orally or by radio and – below battalion level – only orally or by radio. (3) German motorized troops are organized to fight in battle groups with constantly changing organizations – sometimes even daily. (4) During an attack over a longer range, logistic echelons should be thoroughly integrated into fighting echelons, including ammunition, fuel and food as well as medical support. (Quoted in Glantz 1997: 239)

The motorized-infantry regiments performed well in respect of the first three of Zobel's injunctions, but the fourth – especially by the end of July – would show the strain as rearward communications lines were stretched to the limit of their capacity, a problem exacerbated by the rapacious daily hunger for fuel, ammunition and a thousand other items that were needed to keep such extremely complex beasts on the road and ready to fight.

A heavily camouflaged example of a typical *Kradschütze*. At the time of their formation in 1935 motorcycle units were the most flexible (and glamorous) aspect of the Heer's move towards the motorization of the infantry; abundantly supplied with vehicles by the large German motorcycle industry, the *Kradschützen-Abteilungen* were incorporated first into cavalry then Panzer (armoured) divisions, and eventually into all the newly motorized infantry divisions. Operationally, they worked as divisional reconnaissance units as well as 'dismounted infantry' (much like the original dragoons), where their main advantage was their flexibility in adapting to emerging situations and the speed with which they could deploy. (Nik Cornish at www.stavka.org.uk)

Soviet

Despite being at the forefront of military technology and theory throughout much of the 1930s, the RKKA suffered a series of reverses prior to the German invasion, notably the 1937–38 purges that saw Stalin and his acolytes carve through all political and intellectual opposition in the organs of state, especially the RKKA and RKKF. Acknowledged to be the Soviet Union's foremost military mind, Marshal of the Soviet Union Mikhail N. Tukhachevsky was the most prominent victim; with him went nearly all the corps and army commanders and the vast majority of divisional commanders. The advanced ideas that had been at the forefront of military debate also fell from favour, and the new cadre of officers who stepped into dead and banished men's boots were too gauche, too dense or too afraid to make much of those principles that remained. For the officers and men in the rifle regiments the purges had little direct effect, as personnel at this level largely escaped the worst of the venom that ran through the higher echelons. The influence was more subtle, but pernicious. In such an atmosphere even relatively junior officers felt the creeping insecurity that was the natural result of such a trustless system. 'Instead of taking pride in responsibility, an officer was well advised to dodge the limelight and to pass the buck. Cadets learned very little about inspiring their men in field conditions. The party hacks, the *Politruks* [*Politicheskiy Rukovoditel*, or 'political leader'], were supposed to take care of that' (Merridale 2005: 62).

The new commanders' shortcomings contributed substantially to the embarrassments of the Polish occupation and the outright disasters of the Winter War with Finland. Though quietly shuffled to one side after those fiascos, their influence remained: mechanized forces were underdeveloped, operational knowledge stagnated, and freedom of thought and independence of action were positively discouraged in favour of strict adherence to detailed, written orders. Such inflexibility was married with political interference at every level due to the re-emergence of the *Politruk*; such men were ideological guardians of the Party's message, who had equal rank with the commander of the unit to which they were assigned, from a division all the way down to a rifle company, and who could overrule that commander's orders if they saw fit. Such 'dual commands' were an obvious disaster waiting to happen, but in Stalin's RKKA the legacy of the purges ensured that all actions were mediated by loyalty to the Party and its leader.

Communications were a weak point of the RKKA even before the invasion; such radios that were available were lumpen, poorly made things, and telephone communications were knotted up in the confusing rifle-corps organizational structure. Orders from the division came to the regiment in formal written fashion, because they were expected to be followed to the letter, without deviation. Indeed, the orders for the regiments and divisions of Lieutenant-General Vladimir Y. Kachalov's 28th Army at Vas'kovo–Voroshilovo tried to take into account the inexperience of the subordinate commanders by detailing not just what Kachalov wanted them to do, but also

The seven-round 7.62×38mmR M1895 Nagant revolver, though obsolete by the time of *Barbarossa*, was still popular and saw widespread use among officers and some NCOs (most weapons crews had carbines or submachine guns rather than pistols as their personal armament). The revolver's most famous feature – its ability to increase muzzle velocity by creating a gas seal between the cylinder and the barrel, using unique ammunition that had the bullet fully recessed in the cartridge in combination with a mechanical action that pressed the cylinder forward flush with the breech when cocking – necessitated slow and methodical reloading, which was far from ideal in battlefield conditions. Such problems were mitigated by the widespread issue of the 7.62mm TT M1933 semi-automatic pistol. The TT ('Tula Tokarev') 33 was a popular, reliable and effective weapon, with a magazine capacity of eight rounds. Issued mainly to officers, it was meant to replace the Nagant M1895, but never entirely did so. (Vitaly V. Kuzmin) how he thought they ought to do it – a desperate and ultimately hopeless approach. The communications available for rifle regiments were basic: 'Radio equipment below regimental level was unheard of, and few telephones were available' (Rottman 2010: 32). Messengers (*Peshii*, or 'runners') were the order of the day for most battlefield communications between platoons, companies and battalions, with verbal orders and hand signals for platoon-to-squad orders.

For officers in the regiment or battalion, the job of leading their men could be daunting. There was a shortage of officers – 55,000 by the eve of war, according to Merridale (2005) – that forced callow men into responsible positions. In some cases, particularly in the regiments of 28th Army at Vas'kovo and Voroshilovo, the officers, freshly commissioned or dragooned from some reserve station or other service, were put in charge of brand-new formations of men who had, in many cases, almost no training at all. They were then expected – within a few weeks – to lead those men against well-defended enemy positions, making effective use of artillery and air support, even though they'd never done it before, or even been trained how to do it. The shambles that resulted was almost guaranteed. At the most basic level – the NCO – the RKKA did little to encourage initiative and leadership: 'Non-commissioned officers were mainly conscripts trained at the unit Regimental School (*Polkovaya Shkola*), with re-enlisted NCOs filling the higher ranks. This was essentially a Tsarist system, which prevented the emergence of an effective NCO corps' (Thomas 2010: 6–7).

ARMAMENT, TRAINING AND TACTICS

German

The Heer's *Schützengruppe* (rifle squad) contained a squad leader armed with an MP 38 or MP 40 submachine gun (SMG), a three-man light machine gun (LMG) team manning an MG 34 and six riflemen, including the *Gruppenführer* (deputy squad leader), each equipped with the Mauser Kar 98k. The *Schützengruppe* also carried spare MG 34 ammunition, hand grenades and a mixture of smoke bombs and demolition charges. The *Schützengruppe*'s firepower was built around the MG 34 LMG, more than a match for the RKKA's DP-28; the Kar 98k and MP 38/MP 40 were comparable to the weapons fielded by RKKA riflemen, certainly in 1941, but in the coming years the increasing reliance of the Soviets upon SMGs would make the Mauser-armed German infantry feel outmatched, especially in close-quarter and urban combat.

The *Schützengruppe* lacked any integral anti-tank weaponry; the largely ineffective anti-tank rifles (one per platoon) had been all but withdrawn and the job of taking on the tanks was theoretically left to the *Panzerjäger* or *Pionier* specialists. As for transport, the *Schützengruppe* would be moved in 3-tonne trucks such as the Opel Blitz or, as the campaign progressed into 1942, in one of a variety of armoured personnel carriers based on the SdKfz 251 chassis. Driven by a squad member – each squad having two or more soldiers

Marshal of the Soviet Union Semyon K. Timoshenko. As the German invasion came thundering over the Bug, Timoshenko gave up his role of People's Commissar for Defence and moved to the chairmanship of the Stavka (*Stavka Glavnogo Komandovaniya Vooruzhennykh Sil SSSR*, or 'the GHQ of the High Command of the Armed Forces of the USSR'), the Soviet Union's high command. From here he did his best to co-ordinate the defence of the rapidly disintegrating Soviet fronts, but the nightmarish confusion of the situation coupled with Stalin's mental paralysis during those first few weeks made the task well-nigh insurmountable. On 10 July he handed chairmanship of the Stavka to Stalin and made for the front in a desperate attempt to stabilize the situation around Smolensk and stop the Soviet Western Front from collapsing entirely. Timoshenko's command of the battles around Smolensk that ran from July to September was typified by his aggressive and ceaseless counter-attacks with whatever forces he had to hand. These attacks were often ad hoc and lacked men, armour, artillery and air support, let alone enough time to be properly organized, but they blunted the Wehrmacht's advance and made the Germans pay a far higher price in men and matériel than they were expecting. (Cody Images)

COMBAT
Schütze, Infanterie-Regiment (mot.) 15

The plate depicts a soldier of Infanterie-Regiment (mot.) 15 during that unit's assault into the heart of Smolensk in mid-July 1941. The hard, constant campaigning such soldiers had endured had worn the shine off their uniforms and equipment; the constant travel over hundreds of kilometres of sandy roads under sweltering skies, interrupted only by bouts of hard fighting, gave the German motorized infantry the look of seasoned campaigners, despite the fact that the invasion was barely four weeks old at this point.

Smolensk, 15—23 July 1941

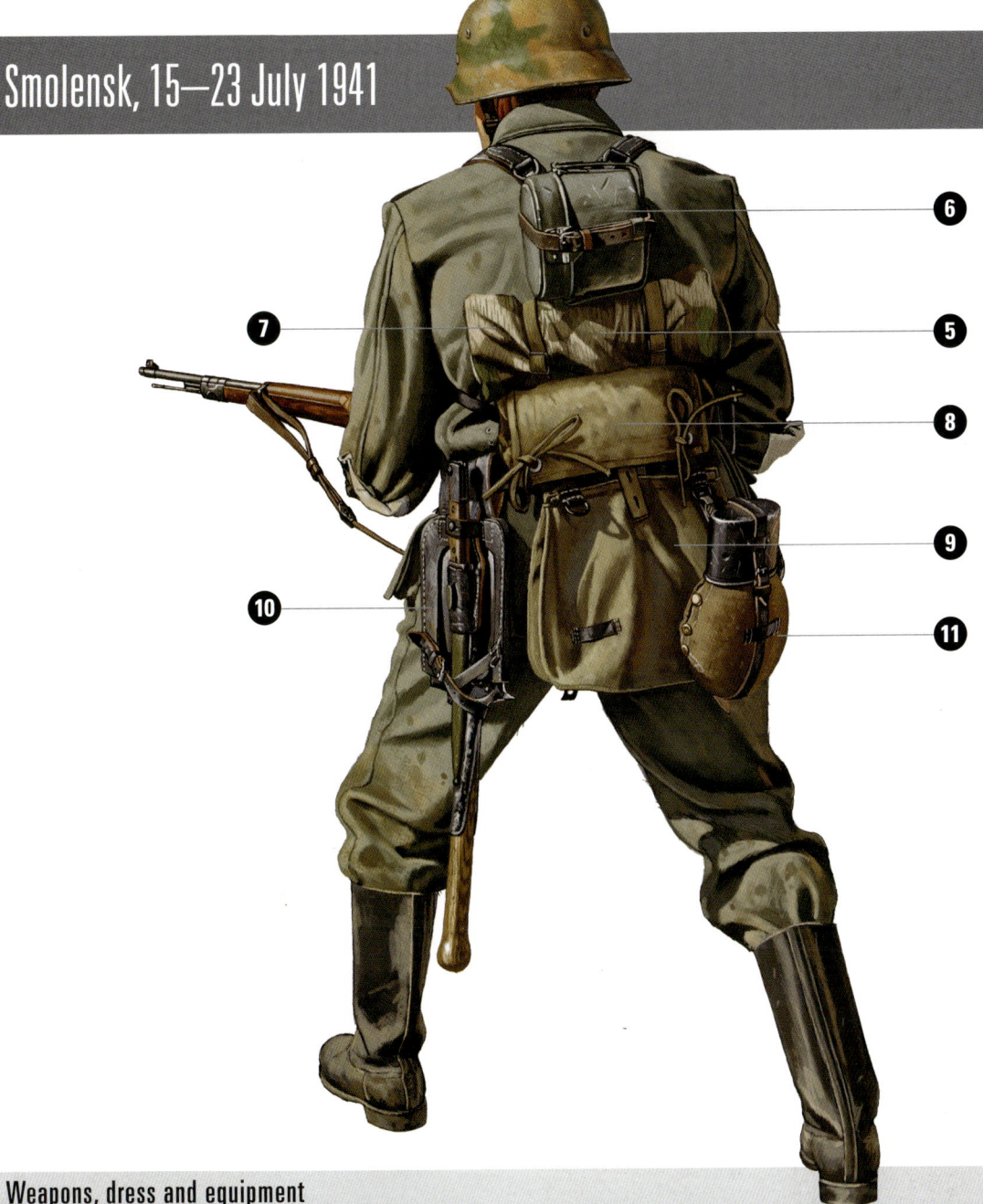

Weapons, dress and equipment

The average German soldier's personal weapons didn't vary greatly from those his predecessor would have carried during World War I. The rifle (**1**), a Mauser Kar 98k (Karabiner 98 Kurz, or 'Carbine, [model] 98, short'), weighed 3.7kg; it was well-made and accurate, but it was still a bolt-action rifle with only a five-round internal magazine. The M1924 Stielhandgranate (**2**) was, with the Eihandgranate 39, the standard German hand grenade of the war, and though its blast was effective it didn't create much shrapnel, leading to an augmentation of its offensive power from 1942 with the addition of a removable fragmentation sleeve (*Splittering*).

All other equipment was attached to the Y-straps (**3**) and waist belt, including the ammunition pouches (**4**), which held a total of 60 rounds (for those armed with the MP 38/40, these were replaced by specially designed pouches holding up to six 32-round magazines).

The *Sturmgepäck* or 'assault pack' (**5**) consisted of an 'A' frame to which the Kochgeschirr 31 cooking pot (**6**), *Zeltbahn* quarter with a *Splittermuster* camouflage design (**7**) and *Beutel zum Sturmgepäck*, or 'assault pack bag' (**8**), were fastened. The Brotbeutel 31 or 'bread bag' (**9**) and the *Spaten* (entrenching tool) and *Seitengewehr* or 'sidearm' (bayonet) in a combined housing (**10**) were hung from the soldier's belt, while the *Feldflasche* (water bottle) (**11**) attached to the bread-bag flap. The M40 *Stahlhelm* (**12**) shown here is hand-painted in summer colours; vegetation, grass or straw was often also used for camouflage, attached to the helmet with bread bag straps, netting or chicken-wire. The equipment shown here (including rifle, grenades and helmet) weighed around 15kg; the soldier's main M39 Tornister (pack) and in this case also his *Tragbüsche für Gasmaske* (gas mask canister) would be left with the company baggage train.

trained as drivers – both types of vehicle offered a pintle-mount for the *Schützengruppe*'s LMG to provide some basic air and ground defence.

German infantry tactics relied upon aggression and the concentration of firepower to overwhelm their opponents. Troops were trained in numerous scenarios as well as in flexible approaches to a problem, meaning that on the battlefield they proved to be capable and adaptable. *Schützengruppen* would approach in a 'rifle row' or 'rifle chain' formation, each man separated from the next by at least ten paces and using all available cover to mask their movement; when under fire, they would advance in mutually supporting bounds, using the LMG to suppress enemy fire. The *Schützenzug* (rifle platoon) followed these basic precepts, usually in a wedge formation: three *Schützengruppen* in a line – the leader's platoon in the centre – with another *Schützengruppe* either ahead of the line's centre as a vanguard or to its rear in reserve. The same wedge/inverted wedge principles applied to the *Infanterie-Bataillon*.

Unlike ordinary infantry, however, motorized infantry were also trained 'to alternate rapidly between fighting from carriers and fighting on foot, and also to combine these two methods of combat' (US Army 1942: 1). At this stage of the war the vast majority of motorized infantry were truck-borne, the SdKfz 251s mainly going to the *Schützen* of the Panzer divisions; even so, the general tactics for manoeuvre and assault were similar, though the stand-off distance and need for decent cover for trucks were obviously greater. The first principle of attack for motorized infantry was always to use 'speed to deliver surprise blows against the enemy flanks and rear, and to penetrate known weak points in the enemy line' (US Army 1942: 24).

Half a dozen soldiers armed with an MG 34 huddle in cover behind a PzKpfw 35(t); 244 of these lightly armed and armoured tanks went into the German bag after the fall of Czechoslovakia in 1938. The PzKpfw 35(t) was pressed into service in Poland and France, though in *Barbarossa* the harsh conditions and a lack of spare parts meant that their numbers dwindled rapidly, with the few remaining operational vehicles being withdrawn in 1942. The ubiquitous Wehrmacht machine gun, the 7.92×57mm MG 34, weighing 12.1kg and with a rate of fire of 800–900 rounds per minute, served (as shown here) as a primary squad LMG, company heavy machine gun (HMG), vehicle-mounted (primary, secondary or co-axial) armament and anti-aircraft gun. Fed with 50- or 250-round belts, it could also accommodate a 50-round single or 75-round saddle drum; for its HMG role it was fixed to a tripod, the Lafette 34, allowing it to engage in sustained direct and indirect fire. Extremely well made, the MG 34 was relatively complex and expensive, leading to the development of the MG 42 – a simpler, more brutal weapon – as a replacement, though the MG 34 could be found in all theatres until the very end of the war. (Cody Images)

Mobility was to be employed to hasten reserves moving into action as well as pulling troops out of thorny situations, and to ensure that fire support from infantrymen and assault guns could be concentrated quickly on the understanding that a 'rapid and determined onslaught is the basis of success' (US Army 1942: 25); to this end they usually had *Panzerjäger* elements attached to the flanks of the leading companies, with heavy weapons and assault guns following close behind to allow timely support. Assuming an attack was successful, pursuit was to be immediate and relentless. The outflanking manoeuvre of IR 20 at Zhlobin followed this model, moving along the southern flank of the town with the 5cm PaK 38 guns of a company from PzJgAbt 10 in close support and the armour of II./PzRgt 6 following behind: the initial advance of the infantry was held up by an armoured train but the *Panzerjäger* knocked it out, allowing IR 20 and II./PzRgt 6 to push through into the town's undefended southern edge.

Defensive tactics were less well executed; the German handbook on motorized-infantry methods gives barely a page to defensive situations, mostly consisting of desultory mentions of outposts and frontages. The deficiencies in such knowledge were thrown into sharp relief in the formation of the *Kessel* (literally 'cauldron'), where the motorized infantry were expected to form an inner and outer defensive ring to stop break-outs or rescue operations, and later on in the battles around Smolensk when the Wehrmacht felt the full force of determined Soviet counter-attacks. A young *Leutnant* from Infanterie-Regiment (mot.) *Großdeutschland* recalled from that time: 'The battalion had taken up a so-called security line spread improbably far apart. This was something new for us; we had never practised it. There was no defence, only security. But what if the enemy launched a strong attack?' (quoted in Kershaw 2010: 229).

German infantry riding on the back of a PzKpfw III (Ausf H or J, armed with the 5cm KwK 38 L/42 gun), passing a machine-gunner's assistant lugging a 13kg ammunition box (*Patronenkasten*) and an MG 34 spare-barrel holder (*Laufschutzer 34*). A major strength of motorized infantry was their capacity to adapt at a moment's notice to a new tactical situation; ad hoc units (*Kampfgruppen*, or 'battle groups') made up of infantry, artillery, anti-tank, Panzer and motorcycle troops plus armoured cars and assault guns were the norm rather than the exception, and were drawn together based on the immediate requirements of the parent division or corps. The high level of training and experience that these units had undergone ensured that they could slip in and out of such battle groups with ease, providing an impressive level of combined-arms interoperability. (Nik Cornish at www.stavka.org.uk)

COMBAT
Rifleman, 457th Rifle Regiment

The plate depicts a notably well-equipped RKKA rifleman serving in 129th Rifle Division as part of Major-General A.M. Gorodniansky's battle group during that unit's defence of Smolensk in mid-July 1941. The 129th was from the North Caucasus Military District and, like many divisions pulled together to compensate for the enormous losses suffered by the first echelon of Soviet armies in the border battles, had rapidly increased its size with drafts of reservists and new recruits to try to bring it at least some way towards its expected wartime establishment.

Smolensk, 15–23 July 1941

Weapons, dress and equipment

Despite the advent of the semi-automatic SVT-40 rifle and the supposed allocations of the PPD-38/40 submachine gun, the Red Army was overwhelmingly equipped with the Mosin-Nagant M1891/30 bolt-action rifle (**1**). Like its German equivalent, this weapon was limited to a five-round magazine; unlike the Kar 98k, it was notable for its length – 123.2cm compared to the Mauser's 110.1cm.

Uniforms were available in summer or winter versions, though in practice the distinctions were often blurred, with winter jackboots being as common as summer puttees (**2**) in both seasons. The M35 *gymnasterka* summer tunic (**3**) and M35 summer breeches (**4**) could be khaki, olive green, olive drab or a variety of interleaving shades, depending on the vagaries of the manufacturer and the level of wear the garments had endured. The collar tabs (**5**), raspberry piped black to indicate the infantry branch, together with the enamel-on-brass branch insignia – crossed rifles over a target – were in the process of being either muted (the raspberry patches giving way to olive drab) or phased out entirely (the insignia).

The cartridge pouches (**6**) were carried on the belt and in total held 40 rounds of ammunition; the canvas ammunition bandolier (**7**) contained 14 five-round clips and was worn across the shoulder. The rest of the rifleman's personal equipment was kept in his backpack (**8**), like the Model 39 version shown here, or rolled inside his greatcoat and shelter cape that was worn as a bedroll across the body. Riflemen would sometimes attack wearing backpacks (either the well-made pre-war M36 or M39 versions, or the simpler *veshhevoi meshok* ('simple backpack')), with shoulder-borne bedrolls, or without either, depending on their personal circumstances.

The gas-mask bag (**9**) usually served as a general purpose carry-all, and the bayonet was almost always attached to the rifle – indeed, the scabbard (**10**) was rarely issued after the start of the war, with bayonets being continuously attached (sometimes reversed with the blade along the rifle's stock when troops were moving by train, for example).

The helmet (**11**) is an SSch-40; at this stage of the war the SSch-40 was seen in conjunction with the earlier SSch-39 and M36 models, though for the most part the riflemen seemed to prefer to wear the M35 *Pilotka* (forage cap) in and out of the front line. Altogether, the load shown here is likely to have weighed 22–24kg.

German *Pioniere* in the process of constructing a pontoon bridge balanced on medium-sized *Schlauchbooten* (inflatable boats). Bridges across the Dnieper were heavily defended and usually destroyed by the Soviets to deny their use to the enemy, necessitating forced river crossings that were fraught with danger; 29. Infanterie-Division (mot.), for example, began its crossing of the Dnieper at Kopys at 0515hrs on 11 July under severe pressure from enemy aerial attacks and artillery fire. Even so, the Germans moved four battalions across the river in 45 minutes, digging in on the eastern bank for the first time, but not without cost, losing a number of men – including some effective and popular officers whose absence would be felt in the coming days. (Nik Cornish at www.stavka.org.uk)

Soviet

The attitude that the Soviet soldier was meant to cultivate towards his enemy was expressed in a forthright manner in Part 2 of the 'General Principles' of the 1937 Provisional Field Service Regulations (*Predvaritel'naya polevoy sluzhby Pravila*) of the RKKA, namely that: 'The constant urge to get to grips with the enemy, with the aim of destroying him, must lie at the basis of the training activity of every commander and soldier of the Red Army. Without special orders to this effect the enemy must be attacked boldly and with dash wherever he is discovered' (quoted in Clark 1985: 43). Such straightforward instruction was in keeping with the training received by the men of the rifle divisions in the run-up to the war – ideologically driven and aggressive, but short on depth and practical experience.

By 1941 the basic infantry unit was an 11-man squad, containing a squad leader, a two-man LMG team, two submachine-gunners and six riflemen. The squad leader, LMG assistant and the riflemen were each armed with the M1890/30 Mosin-Nagant rifle, or – supplies permitting – the SVT-40 semi-automatic rifle; the LMG gunner carried a DP-28 light machine gun, and the submachine-gunners carried PPD-38/40s. Though the weaponry listed hardly seems excessive, the severe shortages afflicting the RKKA through the late 1930s and early 1940s meant that only the prospect of combat would lead to most squads getting their full complement of weapons, not to mention ammunition. The Mosin-Nagant, though dependable and popular, was too long and cumbersome, especially when the bayonet was fitted (as in most cases it permanently was), and the SVT-40 had a range of issues that made it a far from popular choice with the troops. The submachine guns were serviceable, if rather too complex to produce in the required quantities, but the DP-28 was a solid enough LMG.

Training was unimaginative, basic and hard, mostly involving rote-learning, drill and digging entrenchments. The ethnic and linguistic mix of the recruits was not catered for, all instruction being given in Russian, with many blows to help the lessons stick. Weapons training was patchy due to shortages

A Soviet soldier prepares to fire an RM-40 50mm mortar. Weighing 9.3kg (12.1kg while in carry), the RM-40 – one of a series of light mortars beginning with the RM-38, then RM-39, RM-40 and the somewhat different RM-41 – fired an 0.85kg shell up to 800m. Two or three 50mm mortars would be issued to each rifle company, though the small charge (little better than a hand grenade) limited its effectiveness and ultimately led to the end of its production by 1943. (From the fonds of the RGAKFD in Krasnogorsk via Stavka)

of guns and ammunition, with most recruits gaining only the most basic understanding of the tools of their trade. The other skills expected of a rifleman were covered too: 'bayonet, fire against aircraft, actions against tanks, scouting, observing and reporting information, duties in outposts, messenger duties, chemical defence, guard duty, field sanitation, first-aid, camouflage, field fortifications, and breaching obstacles' (Rottman 2007: 14). The training promoted obedience of orders and the men who issued them, with no room for personal interpretation.

Squads would move in a 'chain', a single-file column, each man separated from the next nearby by one or two paces (or up to eight paces in open order). For attack the column would manoeuvre into a skirmish line and then assault as one, with no bounding or fire-and-manoeuvre tactics, support coming from other squads or platoons:

> When the platoon had closed in and was able to make its final assault rush, the troops were ordered to ensure that weapons were fully loaded and grenades

Weighing in at 11.9kg with a 47-round pan magazine, the DP-28 machine gun – known as the *proigryvatel* (literally 'record player'), owing to the shape of the magazine and the fact that it turned as the gun was fired – was roughly equivalent to a German squad's MG 34 in size and weight. Its rate of fire was slower (500–600 rounds per minute as opposed to 800–900 rounds per minute for the MG 34), however, and it lacked the flexibility of the German belt-feed system and was prone to malfunctions if not carefully looked after. (From the fonds of the RGAKFD in Krasnogorsk via Stavka)

A BT-7 Model 1937 light tank on display in the Museum of the Great Patriotic War. Though well equipped with tanks, Soviet mechanized forces were more frail than they appeared due to shortages of spare parts and poor vehicle maintenance. They were also in no sense comparable with the German Panzer divisions, lacking the effective structure, training, equipment, experience and battle-tested doctrine of their enemy. Armed with a 45mm L/46 gun and two DT machine guns (one co-axial, one turret-mounted), the BT-7 was a modern design that could hold its own against the PzKpfw II, but poor maintenance and shortages meant that non-combat losses were very high. These factors were compounded by the fact Soviet armoured units were hopelessly outmatched by German tactical and strategic abilities, and 1941 would prove to be a very grim year for the Soviet Union's tank crews. (Vitaly V. Kuzmin)

prepared. On the order, 'Na shturm, marshch!' (Assault, march!), they rose as a body and advanced at a run without bunching up or halting. Within 40–50 yards of the enemy positions they shouted the Russian battle cry, a deep drawn out Urra! ... They fired on the move and, when within range of enemy positions, threw grenades. They closed in rapidly for 'blizhnii boi' (close combat) with point-blank fire, bayonets, weapon butts, entrenching tools, and fists. (Rottman 2007: 16–17)

Such tactical simplicity suited a rough, variably educated mass-conscript army, and with enough training and experience those methods would bear fruit, especially when properly supported. All too often, however, in those first few months of the invasion, the men who found themselves facing the German spearheads were partially or badly trained, poorly led, underequipped and often without machine-gun, armoured or artillery support. The toll this took on them was horrendous, but they held on, and fought back.

Zhlobin

6 July 1941

BACKGROUND TO BATTLE

In early July 1941, the men of Germany's Infanterie-Regiment (mot.) 41 – hereafter IR 41 – were in high spirits; the war in the East had brought them very far, very fast. The regiment was part of 10. Infanterie-Division (mot.), itself part of XXIV. Armeekorps (mot.), forming the southern prong of Generaloberst Heinz Guderian's Panzergruppe 2. They had crossed the Bug River at Brest-Litovsk in the early hours of 22 June 1941 and had since passed the towns of Kobryn and Byten and the shattered city of Sluzk, crossing the Berezina River on a pontoon bridge at Bobruisk on 4 July – a distance of nearly 400km as the crow flies.

Pushing further into the worryingly vast interior of the Soviet Union, the regiment, together with its sister units in the division, was tasked with defending the 'ever-deepening' flanks of XXIV. Armeekorps (mot.), and had suffered its first casualties in a sharp but successful action against a 2,000-strong Soviet force attempting to break out of the Bialystok *Kessel* on 28 June. Choking on dust and dirt in the insufferable heat and plagued by never-ending clouds of mosquitoes,

A rather idealized shot of the type of young officer common in 10. Infanterie-Division (mot.) and its regiments. With its men drawn from across Bavaria, IR 41 traced its immediate heritage to the founding of the Wehrmacht in 1934. Together with its sister infantry regiments (20 and 85), IR 41 was involved in the German invasions of both Austria and Czechoslovakia in 1938. Mobilized for war in late August 1939, the regiment took part in the invasion of Poland and afterwards the battle of France, after which it was motorized, in October 1940, with the rest of 10. Infanterie-Division. Thus by the time the regiment moved east in preparation for *Barbarossa*, it was part of one of the most experienced divisions in the Wehrmacht. (Nik Cornish at www.stavka.org.uk)

A Soviet BP-35 armoured train of the same type as Armoured Train 16 'Bobruisk'. The train had: a PR-35 locomotive; two PL-35/37 artillery wagons, each mounting two 76.2mm M1902 or M1902/30 guns, with a magazine of 560 shells per wagon; and an anti-aircraft wagon mounting an SPU-BP quad Maxim. The M1930 gun could penetrate 49mm armour at 1,000m, making it a real danger for German medium and light tanks. In addition each PL-35/37 wagon carried six Maxims, each 1902/30 gun having a co-axially mounted Maxim, with a further two Maxims placed on each side of the carriage. (Courtesy of the Central Museum of the Armed Forces, Moscow via Stavka)

the regiment pushed on along 'Rollbahn 1', the designated highway that would eventually lead through Bobruisk to Mogilev, then Smolensk, and eventually Moscow. Before such far-flung objectives could be attained, however, the regiment had to cross the Dnieper River.

Winding its way north to Orsha where it turns east to flow through Smolensk, the Dnieper, a significant obstacle in its own right, had its eastern bank hastily fortified by the second line of Soviet armies, desperate to stop the invaders in their tracks. The German plans called for XXIV. Armeekorps (mot.) to flank Rogachev to the north and south, force a crossing of the Dnieper, break through the RKKA's defensive line and advance to the north-east. The crossing was expected to take place on 7 July and to this end 10. Infanterie-Division (mot.) was tasked with clearing the enemy from possible staging areas around Zhlobin and with seizing the two bridges across the Dnieper on the eastern edge of the town. The division divided into three main elements. First, to assault Zhlobin and seize the bridges, IR 41 was to be strengthened with II./AR 10, a company of PzJgAbt 10, and a company of PiBtl 635, an independent *Pionier-Bataillon* attached to XXIV. Armeekorps (mot.); support for the attack would be provided by two battalions from PzRgt 6 of 3. Panzer-Division, each fielding about 40 tanks. Second, to cover the southern flank of the operation in the Kazimirovo–Radusha area, IR 20 would be strengthened by a company of PzJgAbt 10. Third, mopping up between the Berezina and the Dnieper would be AufklAbt 10. As the various elements of 10. Infanterie-Division (mot.) set out on 5 July they had no intelligence of any sizeable RKKA forces in their path, nor any reason to expect that the operation would not go entirely according to plan.

For the Soviet forces, the situation was radically, disastrously different. In little more than a week four whole armies – the entire forward line of the Western Front – had been so severely battered they effectively ceased to exist, and three German army groups were spearing deep into Soviet territory with seeming impunity. The largest of these, Heeresgruppe Mitte, was heading straight for the Smolensk 'land bridge', the capture of which would give it a clear approach to Moscow. Guderian and Hoth's *Panzergruppen* were shearing through Soviet defences at a terrifying rate; frantic efforts were being made up and down the rapidly changing Western Front to try to check the invaders and at the same time reorganize and redeploy the second-line armies that suddenly found themselves at the heart of the battle. To this end formations were moved into positions on the eastern bank of the Dnieper, fortifying themselves and digging in as best they could.

Soviet doctrine at the time was not, however, based on defensive thinking; fortifying and holding the Dnieper line was a military necessity, but the refusal at almost all levels of Soviet command to accept a purely defensive engagement with the 'Hitlerites' meant that a more aggressive approach would be inevitable. The men of the 240th Rifle Regiment, supported by other units from their parent formation, 117th Rifle Division – itself part of 63rd Rifle Corps of 21st Army – would find themselves at the leading edge of a remarkably over-ambitious Soviet counter-attack at Zhlobin. Arriving in the Zhlobin area on 3 July, 117th Rifle Division took up defensive positions on the eastern bank of the river over a 25km front, while maintaining a small bridgehead on the west bank of the river near the town.

The broad strategic aim for Soviet forces in the area was to attack north from Gomel into the flank and rear of the German advance. The 240th Rifle Regiment was the key element of a rapidly assembled battle group (*boyevykh deystviy otryada 117 SD*, or '117th RD Fighting Detachment') – led by Colonel Spyridon S. Chernyugov, the commander of 117th Rifle Division – that was to take the fight to the Germans. The battle group consisted of: three battalions of the 240th Rifle Regiment; the 3rd Battalion, 275th Infantry Regiment; the 707th Howitzer Artillery Regiment; one battalion of the 322nd Light Artillery Regiment; one battalion of anti-tank artillery; combat engineers; the 321st Anti-Aircraft Artillery Regiment; one tank battalion of 50th Armoured Division; and the Zhlobin Armoured Train 16 'Bobruisk'. All remaining divisional assets were to hold their positions on the east bank of the Dnieper.

According to orders issued on 4 July, on the night of 7 July Chernyugov's battle group was to cross the Dnieper, move through Zhlobin and then make for Bobruisk where it would burn all the crossings over the Berezina River. It would disrupt communications and destroy enemy tanks and motorized infantry and, if conditions were favourable, capture Bobruisk. It would then surround and annihilate the enemy operating in the area of Rogachev. However, at 1145hrs on 5 July Chernyugov received orders that set the crossing of the Dnieper for 0200hrs on the following day. Suddenly, at 1330hrs, Major-General Vasily N. Gordov, the 21st Army Chief of Staff, called 117th Rifle Division's headquarters to demand a literally immediate start to the operation. Despite Chernyugov's objections that his division wasn't yet anywhere near in position, the orders stood – the offensive was to be under way by 1600hrs at the latest. Such complications were further exacerbated by the fact that the orders were given by 21st Army's HQ directly to Chernyugov, completely bypassing 63rd Corps' HQ, which as a result played no part at all in the subsequent action.

Though neither side knew it, both forces would be moving directly into each other's path in less than 12 hours' time.

A Soviet anti-aircraft quad Maxim that has fallen into German hands. Originally developed in 1928 by Feodor Tokarev and entering service in 1931, this weapon was installed in the anti-aircraft wagon of the armoured train, though as the image attests it could be mounted in an impromptu fashion on vehicles or at fixed anti-aircraft defence points. (Nik Cornish at www.stavka.org.uk)

Infanterie-Regiment (mot.) 41 and the 240th Rifle Regiment at Zhlobin, 6 July 1941

1 **0100hrs:** The right-hand column of Chernyugov's battle group reaches Kabanovka; the left-hand column moves through Tertezh with forward elements occupying Zelenaya Sloboda.

2 **0230hrs:** The battle begins in Pobolovo; the Germans are surprised and the RKKA forces are initially successful.

3 **0400hrs:** The Germans are driven out of Zelenaya Sloboda.

4 **0630hrs:** The commander of the 240th Rifle Regiment announces that he is surrounded in Pobolovo.

5 **0930hrs:** The Soviet forces are pushed back to Senozhatki, and flanked by I./IR 41 and II./IR 41; Soviet counter-attacks to the north fail.

6 **0930–1300hrs:** Chernyugov's battle group retreats to Zhlobin, losing much equipment in the marshes. By about 1100hrs, the initiative passes to the Germans.

7 **1300hrs:** IR 20 outflanks the Soviet force to the south along the Bobruisk–Gomel railway line.

8 **1300–1400hrs:** IR 41 & I./PzRgt 6 attack from the north-west; III./IR 20 and II./PzRgt 6 attack from the south.

9 **1400–1600hrs:** The Soviet armoured train is attacked and knocked out by PzJgAbt 10.

10 **1600hrs:** Together with the tanks of II./PzRgt 6, III./IR 20 penetrates Zhlobin.

11 **1630hrs:** The Zhlobin bridges are blown on the orders of Lieutenant-General Leonid G. Petrovsky, commander of 63rd Rifle Corps.

12 **1645hrs:** PzRgt 6 pulls out and leaves the mopping up to 10. Infanterie-Division (mot.).

13 **1700hrs–2359hrs:** Chernyugov's battle group evacuates across the Dnieper, under fire from III./IR 20.

Battlefield environment

The area surrounding the approaches to Zhlobin was variable, with small hills and valleys giving way to lower marshland and peat bogs fed by the Dobysna River, especially around south-eastern Pobolovo and the western approaches to Zhlobin itself, with the west bank of the Dnieper north of the town also dominated by swampy ground. The weather had been consistently hot and sunny, with tall growths of rye and other crops peppering the outskirts of most towns and villages in the area.

Zhlobin was the local administrative hub of the Zhlobin district in the north-east of the Gomel region. Given city status in July 1925, Zhlobin, with a population of 5,000–10,000, was the location of a crossroads (Bobruisk–Gomel and Rogachev–Svetlahorsk), an important rail junction (Minsk–Bobruisk–Gomel and Orsha–Kalinkavichy) with two bridges crossing the Dnieper, (one rail, one road), as well as a number of factories, including a locomotive-repair station, a woodworking plant, an oil mill and a brick factory that made the most of the local clay deposits.

Even before the start of Chernyugov's battle group's operation, some steps had been taken to fortify the city against attack, with defensive positions relying heavily upon the embankments of the railway lines, supplemented by extra works to the north and slightly further west of town. The bridges across the Dnieper had been mined, and a pre-existing force supplied by the 275th Rifle Regiment held the west-bank bridgehead, with some small supplementary units garrisoning the town and some of the defensive works.

A Luftwaffe (German Air Force) reconnaissance photograph of Zhlobin's bridges across the Dnieper, taken on 1 July 1944. Though from a later stage of the war, the locations of the two original bridges are shown: 'A' marks the railway bridge for the Bobruisk–Gomel line, with 'B' the road bridge. Like the originals, these later bridges were made of iron and wood respectively. (John Calvin, wwii-photos-maps.com)

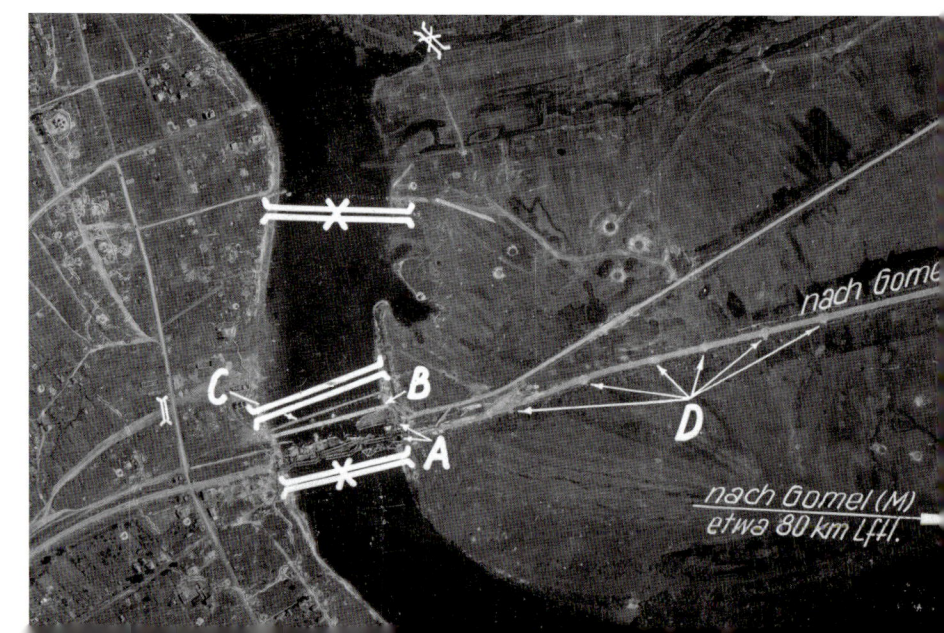

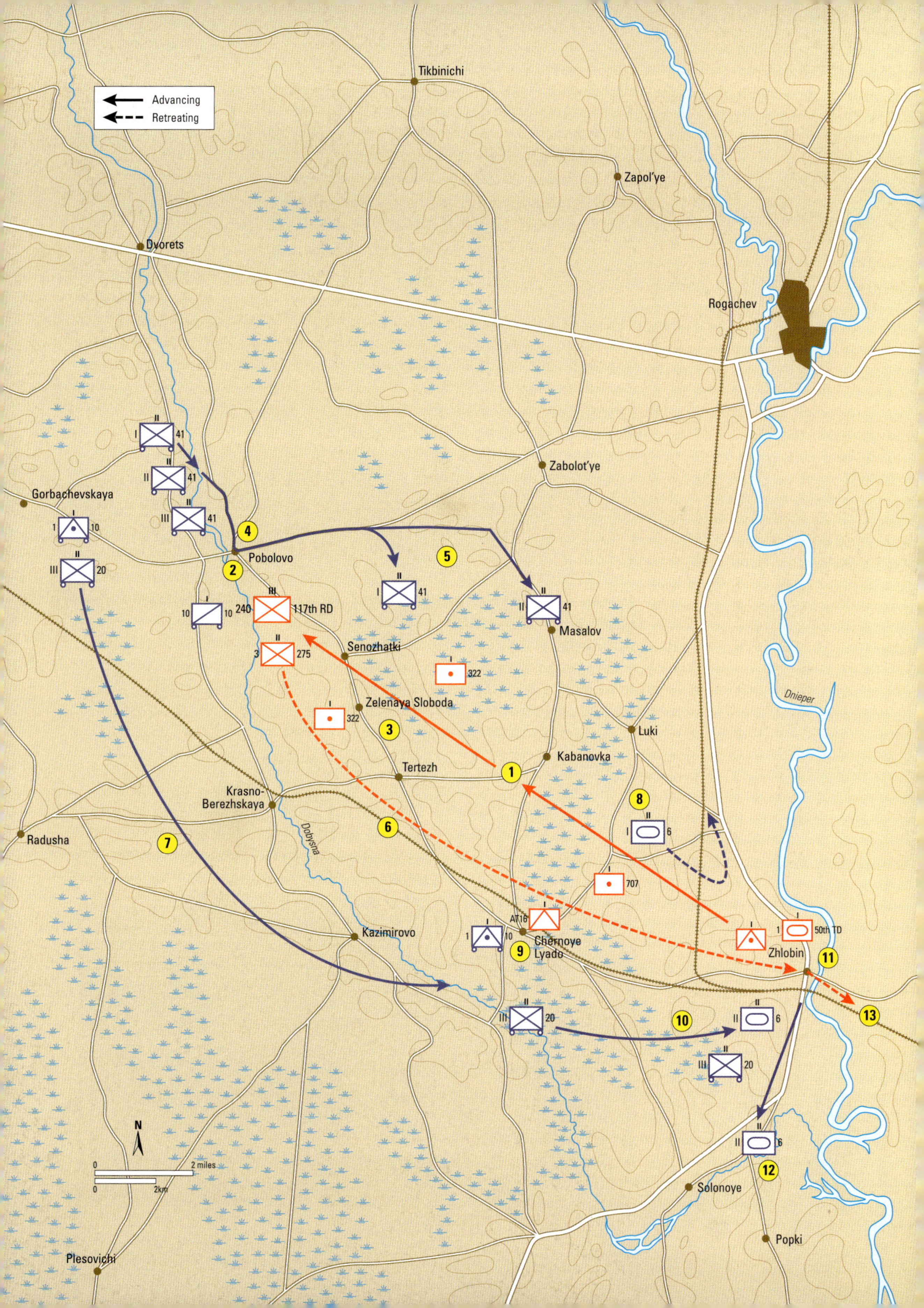

Advancing
Retreating
Tikbinichi
Zapol'ye
Dvorets
Rogachev
Zabolot'ye
Gorbachevskaya
Pobolovo
117th RD
Senozhatki
Masalov
Zelenaya Sloboda
Luki
Kabanovka
Tertezh
Krasno-Berezhskaya
Radusha
Dobysna
Dnieper
Kazimirovo
Chernoye Lyado
Zhlobin
50th TD
Solonoye
Popki
Plesovichi
N
2 miles
2km

INTO COMBAT

Chernyugov's battle group, spearheaded by the three battalions of the 240th Rifle Regiment, crossed the Dnieper and marched into Zhlobin at 1700hrs on 5 July. This force, split into two columns and made up of a confused mix of infantry battalions, horse- and tractor-drawn artillery, trucks and armoured cars, passed through the town and its fortified perimeter, moving north-east up the solitary road that led to Pobolovo and then Bobruisk. There were some inherent weaknesses that would tell as marching turned into fighting; the 707th Howitzer Artillery Regiment, for example, was only carrying 50 rounds per 122mm gun and 20 rounds per 152mm gun, a situation shared by the other artillery units (the 322nd had 40 rounds per gun, the anti-tank battalion had 50 rounds per gun and the 321st Anti-Aircraft Artillery Regiment had 35–40 rounds per gun). The small tank force that had been assigned to Chernyugov was slow getting on the road and was initially 4–5 hours behind the main body, and in addition its tanks (T-26 and BT models) were drawn from training units, highlighting the dismally low availability of front-line armour.

Going was good, though there wasn't much room to manoeuvre as heavy marshland lay on either side of the roadway more often than not. Though no German ground forces were sighted, the Luftwaffe made an appearance, bombing the battle group at 2000hrs, though no casualties ensued. By 0100hrs the right-hand column had reached Kabanovka, while the left-hand column moved through Tertezh with forward elements occupying Zelenaya Sloboda a few kilometres further up the road. The reconnaissance elements of Chernyugov's battle group had only conducted limited tactical patrols, and were therefore unlikely to provide either any significant forewarning of an enemy presence or useful information about the said enemy's strength or movement, a situation exacerbated by the total failure of the corps and army commands to 'fill in' any of these blanks or organize any sort of air cover (supportive or observational). The battle group moved on in relative calm, until Pobolovo was reached a little over an hour later.

At the same time the lead elements of III./IR 41 (mot.) were coming the other way down the road, heading from Bobruisk to Zhlobin, entirely unaware of the Soviet forces to their front. 10. Infanterie-Division (mot.)'s reconnaissance units had probed the area not more than an hour beforehand but had found nothing, presumably missing the advanced elements of

The environmental conditions that the Soviet forces faced were hardly ideal; the area around Zhlobin was low-lying and often waterlogged, with the main roads cutting through long tracts of marshland and peat bogs. To compound the issue the day that the operation commenced was marked by heavy rain that further soaked the ground and made the few available roads more difficult to use. (Courtesy of the Central Museum of the Armed Forces, Moscow via Stavka)

Chernyugov's battle group by the thinnest of margins. Horst Zobel, at the time a young troop commander in II./PzRgt 6 of 3. Panzer-Division, recalled: 'The 10th Motorised Division [...] met strong enemy forces at Slobin [*sic*] on the night of 6 July, despite the fact that its own reconnaissance elements had reported the area clear only 1 hour before' (quoted in Glantz 1997: 393). At about 0230hrs on 6 July, the two forces ran into one another and a fierce fight erupted along the outskirts of Pobolovo, with the initial German forces overwhelmed and reportedly 'massacred and mutilated' (Glantz 1997: 393). For the Germans the surprise of the encounter was considerable, especially considering the immediate artillery and armoured support the Soviet battle group was bringing to bear. A vicious fight developed through the night and into the early hours of the morning, with the advantage swaying from one side to the other.

News of the unexpected encounter started to filter through to successive German units, the war diary of 3. Panzer-Division noting: 'At 3.45 the noise of battle was heard on the right wing, mostly artillery fire. Corps headquarters was informed that the vanguard of 10. ID (mot.) had been attacked by superior enemy forces coming up from the south at Pobolovo' (quoted in Isaev 2010). The response of 10. Infanterie-Division (mot.) as well as that of 3. Panzer-Division certainly confirmed that, from the German perspective, this was far more than a case of clearing Soviet stragglers from the line of advance.

For Chernyugov, barely a third of the way to his objectives at Bobruisk, the situation was moving from unlucky to positively dangerous; his forward position left him far from the prepared defences of Zhlobin, heavily engaged with a motorized division on ground where both his flanks were open. The Germans were making full use of their mobility – while III./IR 41 was heavily committed, I./IR 41 and II./IR 41 took to their trucks and used the roads to move around the Soviet right flank towards Senozhatki and Masalov respectively. Meanwhile, III./IR 20 and one company of PzJgAbt 10, armed with the still relatively uncommon 5cm PaK 38 (the guns towed by either Opel Blitz trucks or 1-tonne half-tracks – likely the SdKfz 10 – that also carried the crews), were also moving, first through open country and then along the road that ran parallel with the Bobruisk–Zhlobin railway line to the south, creating a potential double-envelopment of Chernyugov's whole force.

The Soviets found that as the day progressed they weren't just fighting the motorized infantry in front of them; they had to fend off an increasing number of attacks by small groups of five or six 'tanks with motorcycle troops' that were working their way around their flanks and even into the rear of their positions. Though the harried defenders might have thought they were under attack by tanks, in all probability these mini-envelopments would have been the work of elements of the reconnaissance unit, AufklAbt 10, a mixed battalion made up of a company of armoured cars – employing the four-wheeled SdKfz 222 and the eight-wheel SdKfz 232, both types armed with 2cm cannon and MG 34 machine guns – and a company of motorcycle troops. Adding to the Soviets' woes, the German forces that had flanked their positions to the north began shelling their batteries, the attackers' aim being corrected by Luftwaffe observation aircraft. The result was carnage, with serious losses of vehicles and horses as well as severe casualties among the Soviet battery crews. Ammunition was also running very low – due to a mix of poor planning and unexpectedly

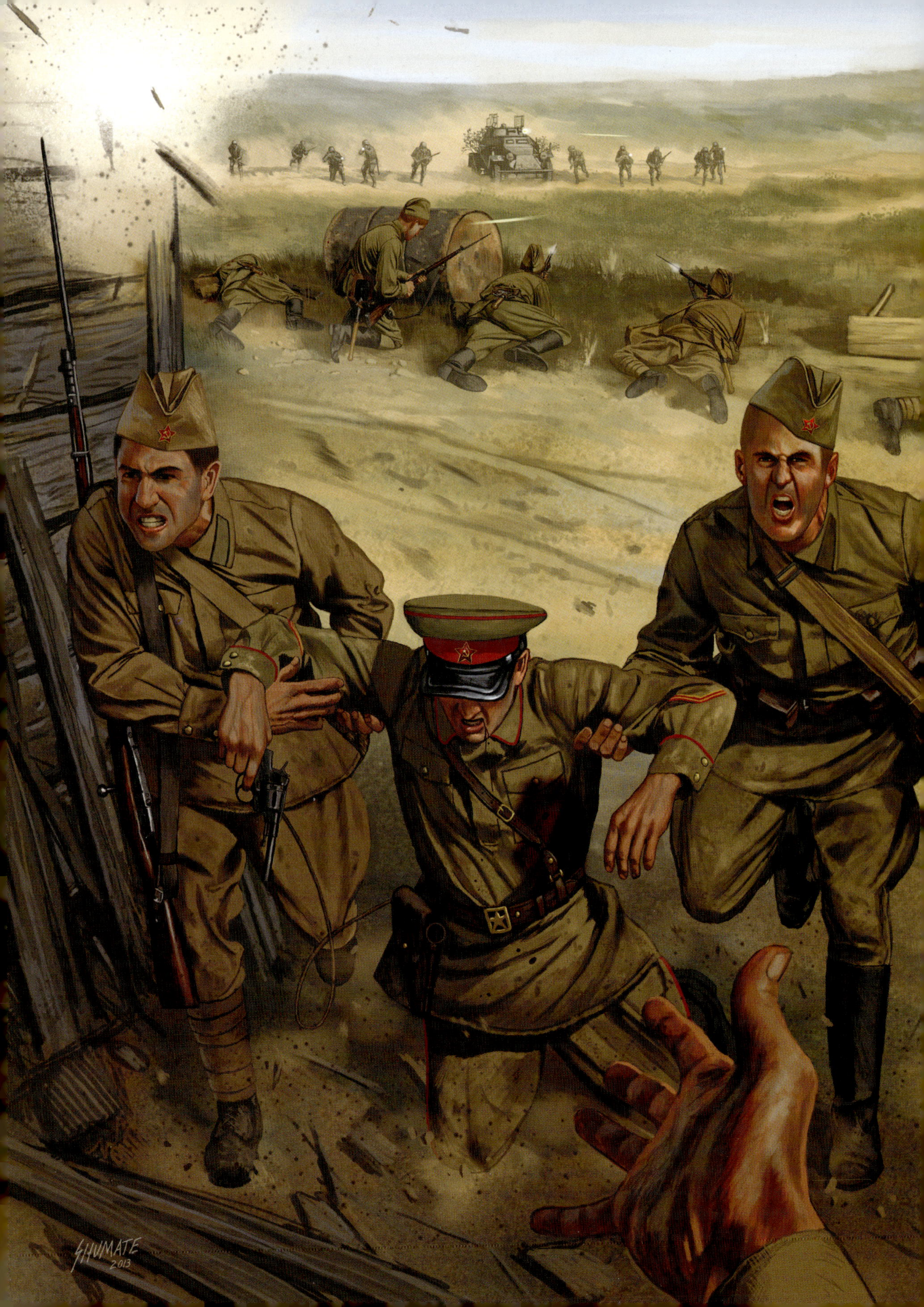
SHUMATE
2013

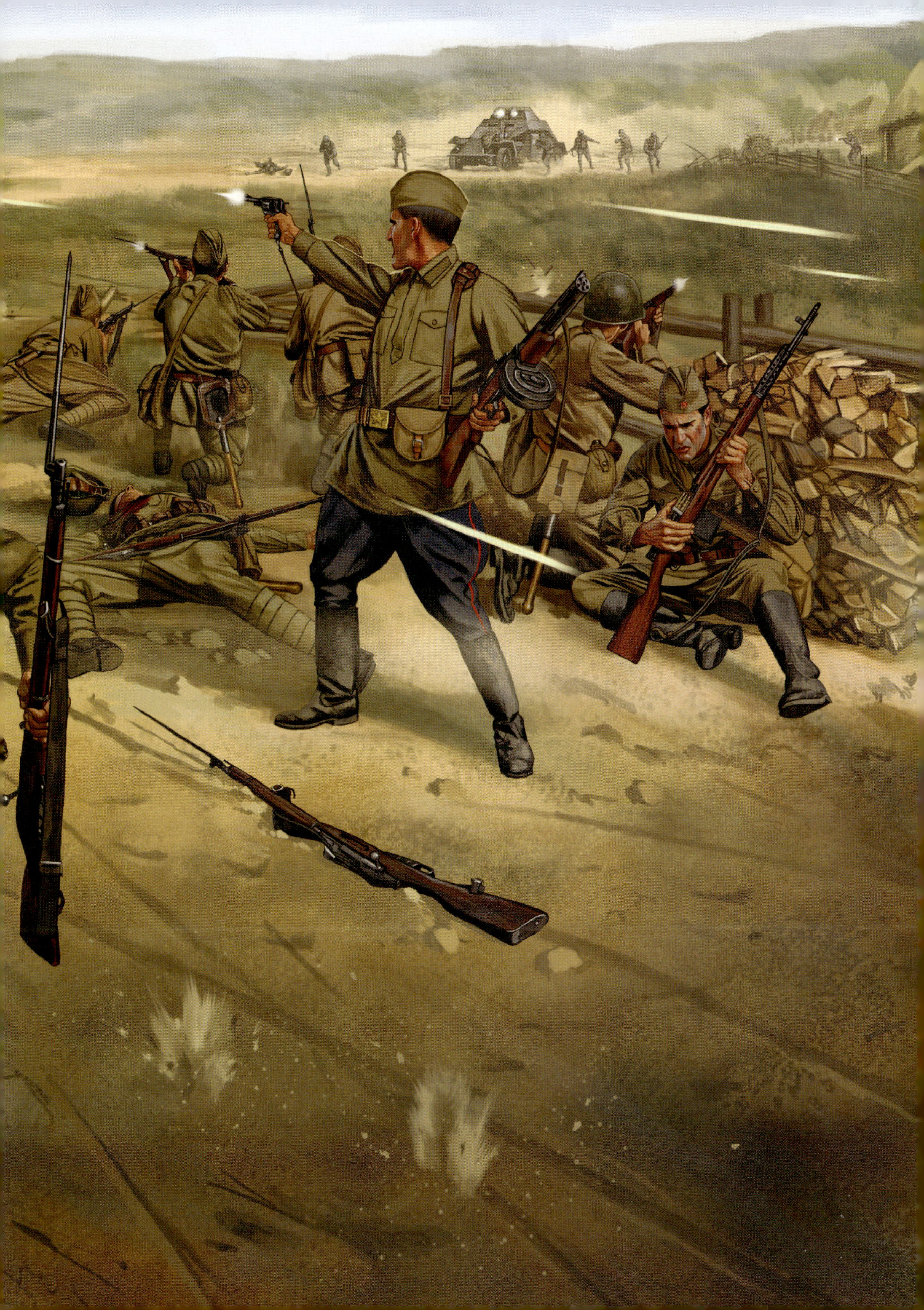

Surrounded at Pobolovo

What started as a victorious encounter has turned into an imminent disaster; Chernyugov's battle group crashed into III./IR 41 in the western outskirts of Pobolovo in the early hours of 6 July, and despite a series of spirited attacks the situation is now slipping out of control for the Soviets, as other units from 10. Infanterie-Division (mot.) rapidly start to envelop his reinforced regiment. AufklAbt 10 carries out flanking manoeuvres with small groups of armoured cars and *Kradschützen*, looping around the Soviet battle group's line and launching numerous attacks, causing confusion and panic. In addition, the men of I./IR 41 and II./IR 41 take to their trucks and swing wide to the north, while elements of their sister regiment, IR 20, do the same to the south, in effect forming a pincer movement closing on Zhlobin and threatening to completely cut off Chernyugov and his men from the town.

Here, the remnants of a platoon from the 240th Rifle Regiment have been forced out of their original positions by the manoeuvres of AufklAbt 10 and are falling back under heavy fire, sheltering by the side of a ruined farmhouse and fighting desperately to stop the highly mobile German troops from overwhelming them. The platoon has been constantly flanked and hammered by the 2cm cannon and MG 34s on the SdKfz 222 armoured cars, supported by dismounted *Kradschützen*. The officer, as all too many junior officers did in these early weeks of the war, has paid the price for leading his men from the front; the sergeant, the ammunition from his PPD-40 submachine gun expended, empties his M1895 Nagant pistol at the enemy. Most of the riflemen carry the Mosin-Nagant M1891/30 and a couple have the SVT-40 (*Samozaryadnaya Vintovka Tokareva, Obrazets* 1940 *goda*, or 'Tokarev Self-loading Rifle, Model 1940'). Though it was semi-automatic and had a ten-round magazine (double that of the M1891/30) the SVT-40 wasn't popular – most weren't well made, and they suffered in the hands of troops whose understanding of how to maintain and use them properly was usually lacking.

The German ethos of attack prized aggression and speed, and the Wehrmacht supplied the men of their motorized-infantry regiments with the tools to drive such attacks home. Against this a Soviet rifle platoon, caught in unprepared positions with no heavy weapons and few natural barriers to hamper their enemy's tactical advantage of manoeuvrability, could do little.

swift German reactions, a Soviet re-supply column of up to 30 vehicles that was critically needed found its pathway blocked by motorcycle troops and armoured vehicles, and had to turn back. By 0630hrs, Chernyugov announced that he was effectively surrounded at Pobolovo.

With the situation critical and total envelopment just a matter of time, Chernyugov started a fighting withdrawal from Pobolovo back the way he had come, to Zhlobin. The ground was not in his favour; to the north I./IR 41 and II./IR 41 and PiBtl 635 had clear roads, while to the south III./IR 20 had an open run along the road by the railway line. Chernyugov, by contrast, had only the wet, muddy road along which he had previously advanced, a road that was flanked by swollen peat bogs on both sides. The battle group had to spread out into this marshy terrain and inevitably the cost in matériel was terrible, with guns, vehicles and equipment of every sort first becoming stuck and then necessarily abandoned due to the constant pressure of III./IR 41 from Pobolovo exacerbated by enfilading fire from the German positions to the north. Soviet attacks were thrown out towards Masalov and Luki in an attempt to check the encroaching envelopment to the north, but by 0930hrs both attacks had been checked and their elements pushed back towards the Soviet line of retreat. By 1100hrs the initiative had well and truly passed to the men of 10. Infanterie-Division (mot.).

The fighting was confused, scattered and fierce, ranging from Pobolovo where the brunt of the engagement was being played out, to Zelenaya Sloboda where the Germans first captured and were then summarily ejected from the small village, as well as sporadic engagements in Senozhakti and Tertezh. Heroism was easy to find on both sides. Feldwebel Johann Jungkunst, a platoon leader in II./IR 41, earned a Knight's Cross for his repeated bravery during the early-morning fighting; a Lieutenant Popov fought his battery with frenzied determination at Sloboda, where, though wounded, he continued firing his guns to cover nearby infantry moving to a new position, finally being killed by shell-fire after knocking out two armoured vehicles; elsewhere Lieutenant Nabokov, commander of the 5th Battery of the 322nd Light Artillery Regiment, was forced to reposition his battery several times owing to the intensity of enemy fire, finally ending up with his guns pointing in all four directions trying to fend off the relentless German troops that surrounded him. Reduced to acting as a gunner due to the brutal attrition suffered by his crews, the wounded Nabokov was one of only six survivors to escape from his wrecked battery.

Unrelenting German counter-attacks had forced the elements of Chernyugov's battle group back on their defences at Zhlobin. Exhausted and battered, they had lost a great deal of the equipment and supplies that they would need to remain an effective fighting force, including scores of artillery pieces, hundreds of horses, machine guns, mortars and vehicles of every type – including over a dozen tanks. However, by reaching the city's prepared defences the Soviets had – at least in theory – given themselves a breathing space and now occupied positions that would be harder for their opponents to flank or envelop.

The Soviet defensive line ran from the Dnieper north of Zhlobin to the railway embankment that provided a consistent barrier to the western side of

The 'eyes' of German motorized formations were the *Aufklärungs-Abteilungen*, made up from a mix of armoured cars and *Kradschützen* (motorcycle troops). 10. Infanterie-Division (mot.) had AufklAbt 10, made up of two companies, one of armoured cars and one of *Kradschützen*, as well as a separate *Kradschützen* battalion, KBtl 40 (made up of three rifle companies and one heavy company). Their extremely high mobility would allow them to play a significant role in the battle at Zhlobin. (Nik Cornish at www.stavka.org.uk)

Soviet gunners man a 45mm M1937 (53-K) anti-tank gun. Based on a German model designed by Rheinmetall in the early 1930s, the Soviet version resembled closely the Wehrmacht's 3.7cm PaK 36, and like its counterpart it was found wanting when it came to stopping enemy armour, often only being effective against the PzKpfw III and PzKpfw IV at dangerously close range. Success often relied upon the guns being well concealed and used in surprise attacks against the sides or rear of German armour, exemplified by the damage such guns helped to inflict upon 1./PzRgt 6 in the Germans' incautious rush towards the outskirts of Zhlobin. (Nik Cornish at www.stavka.org.uk)

the town, with a further outer defensive line at the village of Chernoye Lyado, supported by the armoured train that sat atop the very high berm of the Bobruisk–Gomel railway line. For Chernyugov, the situation was critical; his men had been on the move for the best part of 24 hours, had been denied any opportunity to rest, and had been engaged in near-constant heavy fighting with an extremely capable aggressive foe for over ten hours. The remainder of the tanks (about 30 or so) were set up in defensive positions screening the western and northern approaches to the town, while the men took to the railway embankments or the defensive lines to defend against the inevitable attacks.

By midday the situation seemed ripe for a decisive German assault. The three battalions of IR 41 were closing in on Zhlobin in a semi-circle from the west to the north-west, while the reinforced III./IR 20 was pushing in from the south, but the Soviet resistance was still fierce and was now augmented by the town's strong defensive positions. To crack this potentially difficult nut, the reserve unit, PzRgt 6, was called upon. Two of the regiment's three tank battalions (normally, Panzer regiments had two battalions) were drawn up to the north-west of Zhlobin; they were primarily equipped with 3.7cm and 5cm variants of the PzKpfw III, with a smaller number of PzKpfw II and PzKpfw IV tanks. The firepower and manoeuvrability of these two units would augment significantly the offensive strength of the four infantry battalions deployed by 10. Infanterie-Division (mot.).

Close co-operation between the Panzers and the infantry was not only possible but expected, as both had extensive experience of combined-arms operations with an ever-changing roster of units. Even though the infantry of IR 41 and IR 20 were equipped with trucks rather than armoured half-tracks, they would have been well-used to marking the rear and the flanks of

Panzer units, alighting in cover when within about 500m of the enemy – far enough away to avoid being an easy target, and close enough to give the Panzers the support they would need against infantry and direct-fire artillery or anti-tank guns. In this instance, however, only one of the Panzer battalions would use such tactics. The orders came: Major Gustav-Albrecht Schmidt-Ott's I./PzRgt 6, which had arrived first, was tasked with striking directly towards the town with immediate effect to relieve the pressure on the infantry, while Oberstleutnant Oskar Munzel's II./PzRgt 6 was to push to the south, cross the railway embankment and hook round the southern defences in conjunction with Major Schäfer's III./IR 20. As was the usual way with German operations, once the orders were given and the objective set, it was up to the officer responsible to sort out the details and use his own initiative to get the job done.

The attack of I./PzRgt 6 was split: 1./PzRgt 6 followed the axis of advance of II./IR 41 in support, 2./PzRgt 6 made for the high ground to the south of Luki and got into a shooting match with Soviet artillery positioned there, while Oberleutnant von Brodowski's 4./PzRgt 6 made directly for Zhlobin. Unwisely, Brodowski did not take advantage of the fact that he had several battalions of motorized infantry available for his support, instead proceeding alone, preferring to storm the town in the presumable belief that a quick, sharp thrust would spear through the Soviet lines before they had time to put up an effective defence, letting him seize Zhlobin (and the bridges) in a coup de main. Brodowski's 4. Kompanie advanced at maximum speed, easily breaking through some thinly defended outlying infantry positions and bypassing an enemy artillery battery in their rush to cut into the heart of the Soviet resistance. It was as they came to the outskirts of the town that things went very wrong, very quickly. The Soviets had made the most of the 30 or so BT and T-26 tanks they had left, setting them up in well-disguised ambush positions around the perimeter of Zhlobin, artfully concealed among outlying buildings and the tall rye; they waited until they couldn't miss, then opened a devastating fire on the German armour. No sooner was the first Panzer hit than a second was torn apart by a mine, then three more were destroyed in quick succession by the concentrated fire of the Russian tanks. Facing such odds unsupported, the battalion promptly retreated into the guns of the 152mm Soviet artillery battery the Panzers had bypassed moments earlier, who swiftly knocked out 11 more Panzers. The German infantry, far outstripped by the speed of the tanks, were kept at bay by long-range Russian artillery fire, leaving 4./PzRgt 6

The successor to the underpowered PaK 36, the 5cm PaK 38 was a versatile and effective weapon, capable of firing up to 14 rounds a minute and of dealing with most Soviet armour of the early period, including – when the German gun fired Pzgr 40 tungsten-core ammunition – the T-34. Although it was first issued in April 1940, the PaK 38's rollout was hindered by production problems, so by the time of *Barbarossa* many infantry divisions were still equipped with the obsolete PaK 36 or a mix of the PaK 36 and the PaK 38 – but 10. Infanterie-Division (mot.), like other motorized and armoured divisions, got preferential treatment, its *Panzerjäger* elements (as they were called after their redesignation on 16 May 1940) receiving a full allotment of the new guns prior to the campaign. The guns were towed by Opel trucks or 1-tonne half-tracks that also carried their five-man crews. (Nik Cornish at www.stavka.org.uk)

PzKpfw III tanks take stock in an urban environment. The race of II./PzRgt 6 into Zhlobin was a bold move as built-up environments were very dangerous for tanks, limiting the range of their weapons and offering defenders plenty of opportunities to manoeuvre close enough to wreak havoc. At Zhlobin the complete surprise of the penetration, coupled with the fact that by entering from the southern flank the Germans could take the defenders in the rear, allowed Oberstleutnant Munzel's Panzers effectively to destroy all the remaining enemy armour and force a general Soviet retreat. (Nik Cornish at www.stavka.org.uk)

to fight their way out under the cover of 1./PzRgt 6 and a few Panzers from 2./PzRgt 6. In total, I./PzRgt 6 claimed 19 enemy tanks, 21 guns, three anti-tank guns and two anti-aircraft guns destroyed, but the action cost Oberleutnant von Brodowski his life, as well as the lives of Leutnant von Wedel, Leutnant Busse and 22 NCOs and men. In all, I./PzRgt 6 lost some 22 tanks, with only three of 4./PzRgt 6's 13 Panzers escaping.

The German flank attack to the south was proving to be no more fruitful. The men of III./IR 20 had advanced with relative ease when compared with the bloody efforts their comrades serving with IR 41 had been forced to make, but now they were bogged down near Chernoye Lyado, only a few kilometres from Zhlobin, suffering under the fire of Armoured Train 16, which anchored the defence of the Soviet southern line. The train was proving to be a considerable problem, and would have been a most unwelcome surprise for the advancing tanks of Oberstleutnant Munzel's II./PzRgt 6 but for the efforts of Leutnant Manfred Schwarz, commander of the lead company of PzJgAbt 10, who used his 5cm PaK 38 guns to deadly effect, knocking out all four turrets and forcing the crew to abandon their armoured carriages; Schwarz would be awarded the Knight's Cross for his part in this action.

With the train taken care of, II./PzRgt 6 in concert with III./IR 20 pushed forward against surprisingly little resistance. Racing forward, by 1600hrs the

Panzers of Leutnant Dr Köhler's 8./PzRgt 6 (supported by 5./PzRgt 6 and 7./PzRgt 6) had broken through the poorly defended southern flank of Zhlobin and caused havoc among the Soviet armour that had inflicted such a drubbing on the Panzer unit's sister battalion, destroying 22 of the 30 Russian tanks estimated to have been there, as well as a pair of anti-tank guns. III./IR 20 pushed into the southern edge of the town, while the three battalions of IR 41 attacked from the west and north-west and Köhler's Panzers stormed through the town towards the bridges over the Dnieper. The Soviet line, fatally undercut to the south, couldn't hold, and a general withdrawal towards the bridges began at about 1630hrs.

At this point Major-General Leonid Grigor'evich Petrovsky, commander of 63rd Rifle Corps, gave the order to blow both bridges across the Dnieper, despite the fact that the men of the 240th and 275th Rifle regiments were still fighting an effective holding action against the German incursions. As a result the RKKA troops had to battle their way out of town as best they could, then either find a boat or swim across the river, all under the constant fire from the men of III./IR 20 who had taken up positions on the roofs of the houses and factories overlooking the ruined bridges. Chernyugov, who made it out later that evening by boat, was convinced that the bridges could have been held for one or two more hours, allowing for the rescue of considerable numbers of men and matériel. As it was, the Soviets had some supporting fire from artillery batteries positioned on the eastern bank, though not enough to force the Germans to cease their incessant fire.

By 1645hrs the tanks of PzRgt 6 had disengaged, leaving the clean-up to the infantry. Mopping up in the town and along the riverbank continued throughout the evening and by midnight it was all over. Though the action had been hard fought, the Germans seemed to have much to celebrate – the Soviet thrust against the southern flank of XXIV. Armeekorps (mot.) had been repulsed decisively, with considerable loss of enemy soldiers, tanks and artillery, and though the bridges hadn't been captured by the Germans their destruction wouldn't necessarily slow down the crossing of the Dnieper. On 7 July the men of IR 41 received a visit – and thanks – from both Generalleutnant Friedrich-Wilhelm von Löper, the commander of 10. Infanterie-Division (mot.) and Guderian, after which they and the rest of the division were detailed to the north.

For those of Chernyugov's battle group who made it to the eastern bank of the Dnieper, the aftermath was straightforward; they reported in to their various headquarters, then went back into the defensive positions they had vacated some 48 hours earlier. 117th Rifle Division's operation near Zhlobin on 5–6 July had cost it 2,324 men, or 19.3 per cent of the authorized strength, assuming that all units were fully manned (which was almost certainly not the case – it is likely that the reporting officers used the authorised strength rather than the more accurate division payroll records to hide the fact that the proportion of the losses was even more grievous). This figure included 427 killed, 311 wounded and 1,586 missing. As far as equipment was concerned, it lost 81 artillery pieces – four 37mm cannon, 27 45mm guns, 17 76mm guns, 24 122mm howitzers and nine 152mm guns – plus 49 mortars of all calibres, 148 vehicles of various types, and the armoured train.

For the Wehrmacht the situation was better, though still grim: IR 41 bore the brunt of the casualties, losing seven officers and 116 men killed, and 11 officers and 117 men wounded, with IR 20 suffering the loss of two officers (one of whom was the highly regarded commander of III./IR 20, Major Schäfer), among dozens of others. Of the armour supplied by 3. Panzer-Division, I./PzRgt 6 lost 22 tanks on its unsupported drive into Zhlobin, while II./PzRgt 6 came through unscathed.

For the Germans the battle was not an unqualified success. The losses were heavy – and, in the case of I./PzRgt 6, provided an object lesson in the dangers of tanks attacking without the support of infantry – and were an uncomfortable preview of the bitter fighting that would characterize the rolling battles for Smolensk that would absorb the best part of 50 Wehrmacht divisions in the coming two months. The Soviet forces at Zhlobin suffered from poor planning, the confusion of orders and counter-orders prior to the launch of the operation, the extreme difficulty in organizing an effective attacking force at almost no notice when its constituent parts were spread over a 25km front, the almost total lack of intelligence about enemy strength and dispositions, and the hopelessly unrealistic objectives of the mission. Despite these harrowing limitations, the men of the 240th Rifle Regiment and their supporting units surprised their enemy, fought hard and checked the German advance – albeit for a short while – with their determined resistance.

Smolensk

15–23 July 1941

BACKGROUND TO BATTLE

By the second week of July the divisions of Heeresgruppe Mitte had shattered, outmanoeuvred or pushed aside every defence that the Soviets had put in front of them. The two great claws of the German war machine, Hoth's Panzergruppe 3 to the north and Guderian's Panzergruppe 2 to the south, were racing to encircle Smolensk, which was the key to seizing the 'land bridge' and with it the road to Moscow. For Wehrmacht commanders the advance on Smolensk would become a time of potential trepidation as well as triumph; the vast destruction wrought on the RKKA in the border battles had given way to hard-fought crossings of the Dnieper and the successful breach of the Stalin Line, and yet for most German units resistance wasn't lessening, it was increasing. New Soviet formations were being encountered almost daily and ever more dangerous strongpoints like Mogilev and forces such as Lieutenant-General Vasily F. Gerasimenko's 21st Army north of Gomel were being bypassed, leaving the leading motorized and Panzer divisions with extremely vulnerable flanks and increasingly fragile lines of communication. The German motorized corps had to assume that the slow-moving infantry divisions bringing up the rear would solve those problems for them, as they speared ever onward towards their goal – advancing toward Belyi, Iartsevo and El'nia, encircling Smolensk and trapping all three Soviet armies there in a new *Kessel*.

A view of Smolensk. Dating from 1912, the image was taken on Cathedral Hill on the southern side of the Dnieper. This photograph looks north-east across the river, giving a good view of the two easternmost bridges (the 'Iron Bridge' to the left, with the Dnieper Gate Bridge to the right) that link the southern half of the city to the northern bank. (Sergei Mikhailovich Prokudin-Gorskii Collection, Library of Congress)

German troops in battle order manoeuvre through the outskirts of a town; such work was difficult and dangerous but unavoidable due to the operational limitations of armour in urban environments. As one German soldier noted of such operations in *Barbarossa*, 'It was only when the infantry gained touch that the tanks were safe. The armour may have made its name with the capture of grea towns: Minsk, Bialystok, Dunaberg [Daugavpils], Vilna [Vilnius], but who was it who had to comb the woods and the death-dealing cornfields? Who cleared the hundreds of villages, who cleared the barns and outhouses? The Infantry' (quoted in Lucas 1991: 22). (Nik Cornish at www.stavka.org.uk)

The Thuringians of IR 15 would have been well aware of their objective, as German units were usually kept informed of what their parent division was up to, fostering loyalty and pride in the achievements of the whole organization, not just their own small corner of it. The units of their parent formation – 29. Infanterie-Division (mot.), known as the *Falke* (Falcon) Division – were well trained and highly experienced; raised in Wehrkreis IX in 1936, quickly developing a reputation as a 'crack' unit (according to contemporary accounts it was one of the best mobile divisions of the Wehrmacht), 29. Infanterie-Division (mot.) and its regiments – IR 15, commanded by Oberst Walter Weßel until September 1941, and IR 71, commanded by Oberst Wilhelm Thomas – participated in the Polish and French campaigns, acquitting themselves well. Now they were part of General der Panzertruppe Joachim Lemelsen's XXXXVII. Armeekorps (mot.), together with 17. and 18. Panzer-Divisionen. Lemelsen, who had commanded 29. Infanterie-Division (mot.) from 1938 until the eve of the invasion of France, knew Generalmajor Walter von Boltenstern – its commander – well, and trusted the capabilities of the division's men, making the most of their speed and manoeuvrability.

Guderian's orders were for his units to push on with all speed; to this end 29. Infanterie-Division (mot.) mounted attacks across the Dnieper at Kopys and Shklov, though the crossing proved tricky. The division had to fight hard to get across the river in the face of determined Soviet aerial attacks and artillery fire. At 0515hrs on 11 July Oberstleutnant Hans Hecker's *Pionier* companies crossed the river in assault boats under cover of a battery of assault guns, ferrying the infantry to the other bank. Within 45 minutes four assault battalions had gained the eastern shore of the Dnieper and dug in. By 1600hrs that day the *Pioniere* had built a pontoon bridge and the rest of the division crossed. Aside from a minor diversion to assist 17. Panzer-Division at its crossing at Orsha, 29. Infanterie-Division (mot.) now made straight for Smolensk 'in remarkably short order' (Fugate 1988: 75).

From the Soviet perspective, things were looking bleak. Desperate measures were taken to try to reduce the chaos that the German advance had made of Soviet forces, though 'In reality, the Stavka's wholesale reorganization of the Red Army simply validated the damage the Wehrmacht had already done to the army's force structure by abolishing those elements the Germans had already largely destroyed or had proved ineffective during the German onslaught' (Glantz 2010: 142). The changes, issued on 15 July, would have little bearing on the immediate situation that faced the commanders and men tasked with defending the city and environs of Smolensk from the fast-approaching invaders. Lieutenant-General Mikhail F. Lukin had arrived in the city in early July. His first impressions were inauspicious:

> I arrived in Smolensk by car with a group of staff officers on the night of July 8, 1941. The city was under a blackout – all sources of light were masked. The streets were deserted. There was an ominous silence. This major regional centre seemed dead. It was with heavy hearts that we looked upon the city's homes, wrecked and burned by enemy aircraft. (Lukin 1979)

By 14 July Lukin was given formal command of the defence of Smolensk and its immediate surrounding area by Marshal of the Soviet Union Timoshenko. His main force, 16th Army, was formed in the first half of 1940 in the Trans-Baikal Military District, and currently consisted of one rifle corps fielding two rifle divisions, the 46th and 152nd (though they would later be joined by 19th Army's 129th Rifle Division), and 57th Tank Division. Major-General Alexandr A. Filatov's 46th Rifle Division was initially concentrated in the countryside north-east of Smolensk near Koryavin, Veino and Kolotovino; Major-General Avksentii M. Gorodniansky's 129th Rifle Division was to the north-west; Colonel Petr N. Chernyshev's 152nd Rifle Division was to the south-west; and Colonel Vasilii A. Mishulin's 57th Tank Division was at Krasnyi, south-west of Smolensk.

Few regular forces were available to defend the city proper; there were 'three battalions made up of volunteers, armed only with small quantities of rifles and machine guns' (Lukin 1979). These impromptu formations were manned by workers from local Smolensk businesses and government offices, and were armed with a mixture of Soviet and British rifles as well as Molotov cocktails (hand grenades being in critically short supply). All three battalions were commanded by Major Yevgeniy I. Fadeyev, the former Party secretary of the regional department of the NKVD. Though they were nominally called battalions, in reality they mustered barely a thousand men between them. In addition there were a few reserve and police units of indeterminate quality, as a well as some composite forces; in total they numbered around 6,500 men, of whom 2,500 were in position to defend the city. The city's roads were barricaded, with pill-boxes and strong-points established in numerous houses and cellars, all manned by the ad hoc militia who would soon bear the brunt of the initial attack.

Lieutenant-General Mikhail F. Lukin. From peasant stock, Lukin was conscripted into the Tsar's army in 1913, where his ambition and capabilities saw him gain a commission and – upon the Revolution (when he joined the Red Guards) and subsequent civil war – rise to become a divisional chief-of-staff and a double-winner of the Order of the Red Banner. Staying in the RKKA after the war he rose steadily, becoming the Commandant of Moscow, though he came close to the edge during Stalin's rabid Great Purge, escaping more lightly than many of his contemporaries with a transfer to the Siberian Military District. As war approached Lukin returned to the West, bringing the newly formed 16th Army with him, but the initial stages of the invasion saw little opportunity for anything other than a retreat to Smolensk, already burning from Luftwaffe raids. He would gain a third Order of the Red Banner for his defence of the city, but in October he was shot through the knee and captured, spending the rest of the war in captivity. (Author's Collection)

Infanterie-Regiment (mot.) 15 and 457th Rifle Regiment at Smolensk, 15–23 July 1941

1 **1600–2300hrs, 15 July:** IR 15 enters Smolensk from the south-west and I./AR 29 attacks directly from the south while IR 71 enters Smolensk from the south-east. The German regiments make their way independently to a line near the southern bank of the Dnieper.

2 **0400–1100 hrs, 16 July:** IR 15 and IR 71 launch a joint attack, supported by AR 29 and other artillery units; both infantry regiments gain footholds on the southern bank on the Dnieper by 1100hrs.

3 **0500hrs, 16 July:** Gorodniansky's battle group enters Smolensk from the north.

4 **1630hrs, 16 July:** IR 15 and IR 71 cross the Dnieper in rubber boats supplied and piloted by the men of PiBtl 29.

5 **1730hrs, 16 July:** IR 15 reaches its initial objectives, St Peter's Church and the railway station.

6 **1800–2000hrs, 16 July:** Fighting moves towards Smolensk's northern limits and by 2000hrs the barracks are taken and the northern outskirts of Smolensk are reached. Despite sporadic counter-attacks, by 2000hrs the city is almost entirely in German hands.

7 **0400–1600hrs, 17 July:** Gorodniansky's battle group attacks south-east into Smolensk and makes some initial headway, but is pushed back by the afternoon.

8 **18 July:** Gorodniansky's battle group attacks into Smolensk once more, and is repulsed, only to attack again the next day, this time taking some northern suburbs, and seizing the airfield on 20 July.

9 **0100hrs, 21 July:** 129th and 46th Rifle divisions attack from the north and the 152nd Rifle Division from the west, street-fighting all day; the attacks continue throughout the following two days, with the battle degenerating into a series of 'see-saw' actions, with the same ground won and lost by each side over and over again.

10 **23 July:** 29. Infanterie-Division (mot.) starts its withdrawal from Smolensk, completing its exit in the early hours of 27 July. On 29 July, the last units of 16th Army leave the city of Smolensk; Lukin, realizing that the encirclement of the city is making any sort of defence untenable, has ordered his divisions to withdraw.

Battlefield environment

Smolensk, one of the oldest cities in Russia, had been a critically important axis of attack for invading armies for centuries. Sweden's King Charles XII made for the city in his 1709 invasion of Russia and Napoleon's Grande Armée fought a major battle for the city in August 1812. Strategically located on the 70km-wide 'land bridge' between the Dnieper and Dvina rivers, Smolensk, if captured, would open the way to Moscow.

Bisected by the Dnieper, Smolensk sat on the main highway from Minsk to Moscow and had major rail spurs to the south (Roslavl and Briansk) and east (Moscow), as well as an airport built in the 1920s that lay a few miles to the north-west. The city was home to around 160,000 people before the war, though many were evacuated, with most of the male population joining the RKKA as the Germans approached, leaving about 20,000 to suffer through the battle for the city.

There were three bridges over the Dnieper, the most westerly being the Dzerzhinsky Street Bridge, followed by the Bolshaya-Sovetskaya 'Iron Bridge' and lastly the Dnieper Gate Bridge. The southern half of the city was dominated by the Kremlin walls that encircled most of the town, and by the Cathedral Church of the Assumption (Uspensky Cathedral), sited on Cathedral Hill, about 350m to the south-east of the Dnieper Gate Bridge. All three bridges were destroyed prior to the German attack. The northern part of the city held the railway station (about 500m north-west of the Dzerzhinsky Street Bridge), the civic offices and many of the city's industrial sites. The Cemetery, scene of some the harshest fighting, was at the north-western edge of the city's rail terminal.

A Luftwaffe reconnaissance photograph of Smolensk. Two bridges across the Dnieper are clearly shown (a third bridge that was between them has been destroyed), as is the railway station (marked 'Bhf' – *Bahnhof*) on the northern side of the river, as well as the airfield (with its hangars and runways picked out) that lies to the north of the city. (John Calvin, wwii-maps-photos.com)

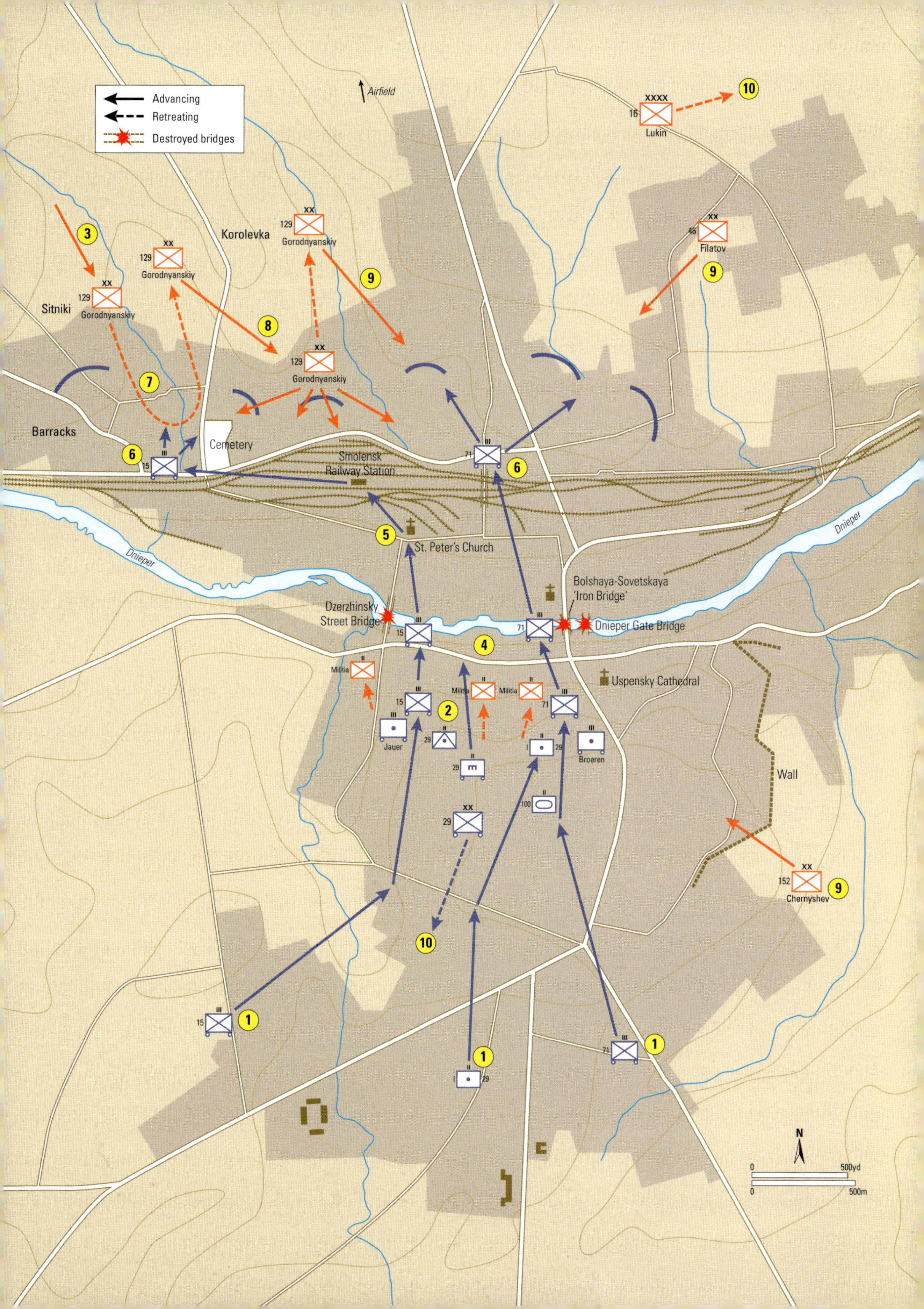

Advancing
Retreating
Destroyed bridges
Airfield
XXXX
16
Lukin
10
XX
46
Filatov
9
129
Gorodnyanskiy
Korolevka
3
8
Sitniki
7
Barracks
6
15
Cemetery
Smolensk
Railway Station
71
5
St. Peter's Church
Dnieper
Bolshaya-Sovetskaya
'Iron Bridge'
Dzerzhinsky
Street Bridge
Dnieper Gate Bridge
4
Uspensky Cathedral
Militia
2
Jauer
29
Broeren
100
Wall
152
Chernyshev
1
N
0
500yd
500m

INTO COMBAT

During the hot, cloudy morning of Tuesday 15 July the Soviets noted the concentrated bombing and machine-gun fire on the roads adjacent to Smolensk, proof of the arrival of the enemy just four days after the western Dnieper had been breached. To the north-east of the city 7. Panzer-Division from Hoth's Panzergruppe 3 cut the Moscow–Minsk road 15km west of Iartsevo and three Soviet armies – the 16th, 19th and 20th, a total of 15 divisions – were cut off. Delivery of ammunition, fuel and food stopped.

The day before, elements of 29. Infanterie-Division (mot.) had been making good progress towards the city until they came upon Khokhlovo, where IR 15 suffered casualties. A quick attack cleared the Soviet resistance by midday on 14 July, but the fighting was fierce and uncompromising. After fighting off a pair of Soviet bombers, IR 15 continued the advance: 'at midday the battle-hardened regiment pushed further forward and by the evening hours of the 15th it had reached the south-western edge of Smolensk' (Lemelsen & Schmidt 1960:122). Oberst Thomas's IR 71 supported by I./AR 29 set out at 0700hrs on 15 July, swinging out to the right to come at the city directly from the south. At 1100hrs II./IR 71 took a Soviet heavy-artillery position on the Koniukovo Hills 6km to the south of Smolensk and, learning that their way into the city was heavily defended, Thomas slipped his regiment to the east on to the Chislavichi–Nikitina–Smolensk road, bypassing the defenders and making it to the edge of town unmolested. Here, 'violent artillery fire' forced a general dismount and the regiment proceeded to attack into the city on foot:

> During the night the shock-troops of IR 71 made it to the south bank of the Dnieper where they paused and rested, waiting for the arrival of their sister regiment in preparation for the attack that would be launched early in the morning … to the left was 'Artillerie Gruppe Jauer' (comprising II/AR 29, III/AR 29, and 1 8.8cm zug from Flakabt 12) with II./IR 15 and III./IR 15, while on the right was IR 71 and 'Artillerie Gruppe Broeren' which included I./AR 29, a Nebelwerferabteilung as well as 1 10cm Abt and 1 8.8cm zug from Flakabt 12. Both regiments were supported by elements of Pz.Jäg. Abt. 29 and Pi.Btl. 29. The separation line between the regiments was the main road that feeds from the south through Smolensk to the Dnieper River Bridge. (Lemelsen & Schmidt 1960: 125)

For the Russians, the German seizure of the southern half of one of their most important western cities in little more than half a day was a blow that had to be reversed. In order to recapture the occupied sectors of Smolensk a special battle group was quickly pulled together based on 129th Rifle Division with some units from 46th Rifle Division and under the command of Major-General Avksentii M. Gorodniansky. The group included the 334th and 457th Rifle regiments from 129th Rifle Division, as well as

Soviet infantry dash from building to building. Street fighting was time-consuming, resource-intensive and extremely dangerous for both sides. The Germans weren't specially trained for such situations, and the confining nature of the Smolensk battle space was an obvious restriction on the capabilities of a motorized force, leaving the men of 29. Infanterie-Division (mot.) with a rather more equal fight than they might have wished. (Courtesy of the Central Museum of the Armed Forces, Moscow via Stavka)

the 314th Rifle Regiment from 46th Rifle Division. Numbering around 10,000 relatively fresh men, Gorodniansky's battle group entered the city from the north at 0500hrs on 16 July, unaware that the Germans were already on the move once again.

By 0400hrs on 16 July all was ready. Both infantry regiments of 29 Infanterie-Division (mot.), supported by AR 29, 8.8cm anti-aircraft guns, assault guns and the flame-throwing PzKpfw II (F) tanks of PzAbt 100, attacked the Soviet positions on the southern bank of the Dnieper. The German approach was cautious and at first met surprisingly little resistance as the attackers moved through the 'dead city'. Unteroffizier Finke from the headquarters detachment of 11. Kompanie, III./IR 15, noted how 'the destruction was even greater than we had seen in the cities of Minsk and Borisov. There were only a few intact buildings, including some party palaces, that stood out from the many still-smoking ruins' (quoted in Lemelsen & Schmidt 1960: 125). By 1100hrs IR 15 and IR 71 had, through increasingly bitter street-fighting, secured the southern bank of the Dnieper, but Soviet aerial attacks as well as artillery fire from the northern bank were increasing, setting ablaze most of the remaining wooden buildings south of the river and enveloping the city in smoke. The German guns were of limited use in direct support of the infantry owing to poor visibility and the narrowness of the town's mostly ruined streets.

All three bridges across the Dnieper had been destroyed in the preceding days by Soviet engineers, so to gain the northern shore 29. Infanterie-Division (mot.) would need to force a crossing. At 1630hrs the main assault was launched, with IR 71 and IR 15 crossing to the north bank in rubber boats 'safely and quickly controlled' (quoted in Lemelsen & Schmidt 1960: 126) by the *Pioniere* under direct covering fire from AR 29 and other supporting

An SdKfz 10/4 half-track with 2cm FlaK 30 in action with infantry alongside in a drainage ditch. Though nominally anti-aircraft weapons, FlaK guns were a very effective – and, in the case of those mounted on SdKfz vehicles, quickly responsive – form of infantry support. As the Luftwaffe had gained air superiority from the first hours of the campaign, FlaK units were often available to lend the infantry a helping hand. Most motorized divisions would have a separate *FlaK-Kompanie* (though 10. Infanterie-Division (mot.) did not at this stage of the war) consisting of eight 2cm FlaK 30/38 and two 'quad' 2cm Flakvierling 38, all mounted on SdKfz half-track variants. As the war progressed the FlaK units evolved into full battalions. (Nik Cornish at www.stavka.org.uk)

German officers enter Smolensk shortly after its initial capture by 29 Infanterie-Division (mot.). The Germans' assumption that after two days of hard fighting the city was effectively taken was soon put to the test by the constant Soviet counter-attacks, drawing out the battle for the city of Smolensk for over a week; motorized troops were expected to bypass strongpoints or seize objectives and move on quickly, leaving their reduction to the following infantry, a pattern that had been followed at Brest-Litovsk and Minsk, but at Smolensk the men of 29. Infanterie-Division (mot.) found themselves fighting street to street, house to house, presaging their destruction a little over a year later at Stalingrad. (Nik Cornish at www.stavka.org.uk)

elements ranged along the river's southern bank. Despite significant Soviet shelling the 'magnificent' supporting fire they received ensured that both German regiments made it across the river more or less intact (quoted in Lemelsen & Schmidt 1960: 126). IR 15 was detailed to take the railway station, while the men of IR 71 were to make for a widely recognizable white house in the northern part of the town. The hard street-fighting that the regiments had encountered on the approach to the southern bank was a foretaste of the strength and intensity of the fight that they met on the northern shore. Unteroffizier Finke again: 'shots poured out from every corner, every cellar. Everywhere the Soviets had to be smoked out of their hiding places, which they defended tenaciously. In addition the enemy's artillery fire was becoming increasingly accurate. All around us fires raged. Most of the city was made up of thatched wooden houses, which went up like matches' (quoted in Lemelsen & Schmidt 1960: 126). The fighting was unrelenting and vicious, punctuated by increasingly fervent artillery bombardments. A cemetery became the focus of a short, intense struggle:

> In Smolensk, the enemy was able to cross to the north bank of the Dnieper and into the cemetery controlled by the 129th Infantry Division [*sic*] (commanded by Major-General A.M. Gorodniansky), beginning a bloody battle. The cemetery's tombstones, stone monuments, and crypts served as good hiding places for the soldiers. They offered stubborn resistance to the enemy. Suffice it to say that the north-western part of the Smolensk cemetery had changed hands three times in the fighting. But the now-weakened units of the division were unable to deter attacks by their more numerous enemies, who were using tanks, mortars and flamethrowers in large quantities. [By the end of] July 16 the division had retreated to the north-western outskirts of the city. (Lukin 1979)

By 1800hrs both regiments had taken their objectives and moved on, approaching the northern outskirts of the city, with Unteroffizier Finke's *Kompanie* at the forefront: 'The nearer we approached the northern edge, the stronger the enemy artillery fire became … Shells were bursting constantly. It was a real witch's cauldron' (quoted in Lemelsen & Schmidt 1960: 124). Further problems were thrown up by some 'military barracks with well-dug-in field fortifications that proved to be a tough nut to crack' (Fugate 1988: 79). Yet crack it they did, clearing roads and houses with automatic weapons, grenades and flamethrowers as they went. They battered the defenders, mostly men from the 334th and 457th Rifle regiments of Gorodniansky's 129th Rifle Division, pushing them out of the city so that by 2000hrs Smolensk was effectively taken. This did not stop the fighting, however. Well-entrenched Soviet artillery positions on the hills to the north rained down incessant fire and several waves of infantry counter-attacks had to be cut down with machine-gun fire, while a series of tank assaults had to be fought off by the division's *Panzerjäger* elements. By nightfall, according to Finke, the 'scary red reflection of countless fires hung over the city, chasing away the darkness' (quoted in Lemelsen & Schmidt 1960: 126).

The following day PiBtl 29 attempted to rebuild the city's wrecked bridges, but their position was easy to target for the Soviet batteries on the northern hills, and the *Pioniere* suffered heavy losses. IR 15 held the north of the city, IR 71 the north-east; both were to endure six days of Soviet counter-attacks that aimed to wrest the city from their grasp. The Soviet command tried to co-ordinate attacks from the north and the south-east, but various factors caused the postponement of the southern assaults for several days, leaving Gorodniansky's battle group as the most important fighting force in the attempts to retake the city.

For the men of IR 15 and IR 71 the quick success of 15 July that had turned into a hard-won fight on 16 July now threatened to become a vicious battle of attrition. Defensive measures were quickly organized, strongpoints established, and arrangements made for support from other elements of the division. Lieutenant-General Lukin noted how 'in the town the enemy had the support of heavy mortar and machine-gun fire, as well as medium and heavy tanks. Barbed wire was strung between the houses and across the streets, and some houses were mined' (Lukin 1979). Gorodniansky's men pushed into the city with a major counter-attack early in the morning of the 17th, forcing IR 71 and IR 15 to regroup and fight hard to eject them from the city once again by the afternoon. The Soviet operational summary of the Western Front at 2300hrs on 17 July notes that

> Major-General Gorodniansky's Detachment (46th and 129th Rifle Divisions) [are] attacking the northern part of Smolensk, with one battalion, 334th RR, at Karmachi and Sitniki [in the north-western suburbs of Smolensk] 1st Bn, 314th RR at Korolevka and Marker 251 [the north-eastern suburb of Smolensk], and 3rd Bn, 457th RR attacking on its left wing. The detachment attacked toward Smolensk at first light on 17 July … (Quoted in Glantz 2010: 171)

The positions of the units and their attacks are clear, more so than the fact that by the time this report was issued the attack had failed. This was partly due to the difficulties inherent in timely and effective communications in the midst of a massive encirclement battle, but also because Stalin had set the tone for the recapture of the city. Shamed by the quick fall of such an important symbol and embarrassed by his own son's recent capture to the east of Smolensk, 'he accused all the western front commanders of having an "evacuation attitude"' (Glantz 2010: 163) that showed them to be little better than treasonous criminals. Timoshenko, correctly interpreting this threat from above, issued his own stern orders that echoed his master's anger that the city had been surrendered 'too lightly', stating baldly: 'Do not surrender the city of Smolensk under any circumstances' (quoted in Glantz 2010: 165).

Thus it was that the men of Gorodniansky's battle group would have to attack again, and again. 'The battle for the northern part of Smolensk did not cease by night or day, with every street, every house fought over' (Lukin 1979). It wasn't merely a matter of just following orders, though; the energy and ferocity of the assaults launched by the men of 129th and 46th Rifle divisions was due in part at least to 'our soldiers' growing hatred of the enemy: the killed and mutilated bodies of Red Army commanders are seen on the streets of Smolensk, political workers and civilians, including children' (Lukin 1979).

A PM 1910 gun crew moves to a new position. The Maxim shown here lacks its removable defensive plate, presumably in an attempt to alleviate the usual weight of the weapon and its 'Sokolov' carriage (an eye-watering 64.3kg between them). Fed by 250-round cloth belts, the gun had a rate of fire of 600 rounds per minute. A rifle battalion's three rifle companies would each have a machine-gun platoon with two PM 1910s, and the battalion would field a separate machine-gun company (and mortar company early in the war) with a further 12 PM 1910 machine guns. (Courtesy of the Central Museum of the Armed Forces, Moscow via Stavka)

On 18 July, Gorodniansky's men were ordered to resume their attack, this time with their depleted ranks reinforced with some previously mauled units of 127th and 158th Rifle divisions. They tried to force their way into the city's northern suburbs, while 34th Rifle Corps, containing the remainder of 127th and 158th Rifle Divisions, came in from the south-east; these attacks 'scarcely dented' the well-prepared defences of 29. Infanterie-Division (mot.) (Glantz 2010: 172).

Saturday 19 July saw a continuation of the previous day's actions, with the regiments of 46th and 129th Rifle divisions attacking into the north of the city once more, taking ground for a short while only to be pushed back, then taking it once more in a 'seesaw battle' that left them in partial control of some of the north-west suburbs of the city. The report for the end of the day saw the '1st Bn, 340th RR, and one battalion of 720th RR on the western edge of Smolensk and the airfield; 3rd Bn, 457th RR, in the northern suburbs of Smolensk, and 343rd RR (less one rifle battalion) at the Marker 251 line [the north-eastern suburb of Smolensk]' (quoted in Glantz 2010: 175). The next day saw more of the same, with 129th Rifle Division (now four battalions strong) taking the airfield to the north-west of the city, but not much more. At 0100hrs on 21 July 129th Rifle Division was attacking again, fighting through the same ruined streets all day, pushed back by IR 71 and IR 15 yet again; by sunset it was little more than a shadow of its former self, with just four understrength battalions, among them 'the 343rd RR (330 men) at the road junction 1 kilometre north of Smolensk, and 457th RR (470 men) on northern slope of hill 251.9' (Glantz 2010: 179). Losses throughout 16th Army were acknowledged to be at 40 per cent, though the constant fighting in the city almost certainly caused higher losses among the units that were engaged there: 'at the start of the war each of our divisions was six to seven thousand men strong, but after days of fighting this number had fallen to between one and two thousand, with some units of the 16th Army unable to field more than a hundred men' (Lukin 1979).

For IR 15 and IR 71 these days were a period of intense strain. The constant attacks compelled unending vigilance, leading to exhaustion. The attacks themselves were violent and often prolonged, involving active street-fighting to push the Soviets back. Artillery support was vital and in constant demand, yet due to supply problems the stocks of ammunition were running critically low, causing the use of the guns to be rationed. Though the Soviet artillerists were in a similarly straitened situation as their German counterparts, it didn't seem that way to those on the receiving end of their efforts. Karl Spahn, a German soldier captured during the battle, said: 'Fighting at Smolensk was the hardest I've ever taken part in … [a] continuous artillery duel … practically wiped out everybody on both sides … I don't see how any of us ever survived that terrible hell at Smolensk' (quoted in Cohen 2013: 56). To add to the pressure the new attacks by 34th Rifle Corps (127th and 158th Rifle divisions) on the south-eastern flank of the city also threatened to make headway, necessitating an emergency assault by 17. Panzer-Division on 22 July that would take to two days to break the Soviet threat and 'stabilise the situation' (Glantz 2010: 177). Despite the severity of their losses and the growing crisis of food, ammunition and medical shortages, the Soviet infantry still refused to lessen the frequency or the intensity of their attacks:

> July 22 and 23 in Smolensk saw continued fierce fighting. The enemy stubbornly defended every house, unleashing a mass of fire from mortars and machine guns on our attacking units. In addition to artillery fire there were their flamethrower tanks, from which jets of fire lanced out, up to 60 metres in length, and which burned everything they touched. The Luftwaffe bombed us incessantly each day. A strong battle continued to be fought at the cemetery, which the 152nd Infantry Division occupied twice (it had earlier been taken by the 129th Infantry Division three times). Fighting for the cemetery, for each stone, each building, was savage and often came down to a hand-to-hand struggle, which almost always ended in success for our troops. The onslaught was so strong that the Nazis of the 29th Motorised Division were unable to carry away their dead and seriously wounded ... (Lukin 1979)

By this point the strategic situation called for the motorized capabilities of 29. Infanterie-Division (mot.) elsewhere, so a staged withdrawal was organized, starting on 23 July; the last units left on the night of 26/27 July, replaced by those from the newly arrived 137. Infanterie-Division. It was on the night of 27 July that the noose around the Smolensk *Kessel* was finally drawn tight, necessitating some quick decision-making from Lieutenant-General Lukin and the commanders of the other trapped armies. For Lukin, at least, the answer was obvious:

> The leaders of my divisions – P.N. Chernyshev of the 152nd, A.M. Gorodniansky of the 129th and A.A. Filatov of the 46th – were disciplined commanders tested in heavy fighting, and without my orders they would never have left Smolensk. The units and formations of the 16th Army were withdrawn on my orders, because by this point they had exhausted all their opportunities for resisting the enemy. In these divisions there were literally only two or three hundred men remaining, most of

A Soviet LMG team setting up a DT (*Degtyaryova Tankovy*) with a 60-round pan magazine in a prepared defensive position. The DT was a vehicle-borne variant of the DP-28 squad support weapon, and although heavier than the DP-28 it had the advantage of a larger magazine as well as a heavier barrel that allowed for more sustained fire. Despite its design as a vehicle-mounted weapon it wasn't uncommon, certainly at this stage of the war, to find DTs pressed into infantry service. (From the fonds of the RGAKFD in Krasnogorsk via Stavka)

whom had neither grenades nor ammo. Such remnants of divisions would be easy prey for the Nazis. So I gave the order to leave Smolensk. At the time there was no other choice. (Lukin 1979)

The last units of 16th Army left Smolensk on the night of 29 July. Their respite was short; subsumed by 20th Army, they would fight on until they were destroyed in the Vyazma *Kessel* a few months later.

The cost of the fight for the city of Smolensk was very high. The city itself was reduced to a smoking ruin, as recorded by a correspondent for the Spanish newspaper *ABC*, Miguel Arena: 'Almost nothing remains of Smolensk from the first bombs by the Germans and the large fires set by the retreating Red Army … These attacks have left the city as not much more than a skeleton. The city is a heap of rubble…left standing are Hotel Smolensk, the State bank, and the cathedral turned museum' (quoted in Cohen 2013: 59). Despite Stalin's initial exhortations to retake the city at all costs, the larger strategic realities of the situation forced him to accept its loss, as well as the horrendous casualties that accompanied it – more than 309,000 men in the defence of the *Kessel*, and around 760,000 men for the whole period of the battle (10 July–10 September). Despite this, the RKKA had, unlike in previous encirclements, remained an effective fighting force, with good leadership and relatively contiguous lines allowing the units to retain cohesion and drag the fight out far longer than the Germans wanted. Generaloberst Franz Halder, the *Chef des Generalstabes des Heeres* (Army Chief of Staff), noted the Soviet resistance at Smolensk was 'fanatic and dogged' (Erickson 1983: 174), and he wasn't the only one who had noticed; many German officers were starting to re-evaluate their preconceived ideas of the fighting capabilities of the Soviet soldier.

For the Germans, the relative lack of substantial infantry formations meant the brunt of the fight had to be absorbed by Panzers and motorized-infantry regiments. 29. Infanterie-Division (mot.) had captured the city quickly, but found themselves stuck for the best part of ten days in the middle of a shattered city, fighting a savage battle of attrition, where their best operational asset – their mobility – counted for very little. 29. Infanterie-Division (mot.) lost more men than any other formation in Panzergruppe 2 in the period 14–19 July: 185 men killed, 795 wounded and eight missing, for a total of 988 men, a significant percentage of the division's fighting strength. The stress and intensity of the combat they had endured left a lasting impression on the men who fought there. Fritz Ehr, taken prisoner during the battle, said, 'I don't want to be in any more battles like the one at Smolensk. I wouldn't live through another like that. The Russians almost killed every one of us at Smolensk … That fighting at Smolensk was like hell' (quoted in Cohen 2013: 56). Generalmajor Walther Nehring, the commander of 18. Panzer-Division, had already noted before the advance on Smolensk that the level of casualties could not be maintained 'if we do not intend to win ourselves to death' (quoted in Glantz 2010: 159). The invaders had come over 700km since 22 June; Moscow was only 350km away. But Smolensk warned the Germans that from here the going would be slower, and much harder.

Generalmajor Walter von Boltenstern receiving his Knight's Cross for outstanding leadership on 13 August 1941 from the commander of XXXXVII. Armeekorps (mot.) – and the former commander of 29. Infanterie-Division (mot.) – General der Panzertruppe Joachim Lemelsen. Boltenstern remained on the Eastern Front for most of the war, falling into Russian hands in 1945 and dying in Voikovo prisoner-of-war camp in 1952, while from late 1943 Lemelsen moved on to commands in France and then Italy, fighting defensive battles there until his capture by the Allies; he remained in captivity until 1947, eventually dying in Göttingen, Germany, in 1954. (Author's Collection)

Vas'kovo—Voroshilovo

23–27 July 1941

BACKGROUND TO BATTLE

The RKKA was in crisis. Its first echelon of armies had been destroyed in the border battles, while the second had been overrun on the Dnieper Line and were being crushed rapidly by the encirclements of Heeresgruppe Mitte, most notably 16th, 19th and 20th armies in the Smolensk *Kessel*. Offensively minded by nature, the RKKA rapidly pulled together a third echelon of armies specifically designed to launch a series of massive counter-attacks on the thinly spread German encirclement's perimeter. On 20 July General of the Army Georgy K. Zhukov transferred four armies from the Stavka's Front of Reserve Armies to Timoshenko's Front. These armies would strike simultaneously along an axis from Belyi in the north through Iartsevo in the centre to Roslavl in the south – 'In short, the Stavka insisted Timoshenko's forces encircle the German forces encircling Smolensk' (Glantz 2010: 195).

The centre of the line was Lieutenant-General Konstantin K. Rokossovsky's Group Iartsevo, the four elements of which held

Soviet troops relax next to a train car. The role of the railways was crucial to the RKKA's defence of the Motherland, as the paucity of motorized formations and the state of the roads (good ones were scarce, and the rest were poor and subject to the vagaries of the seasons) precluded rapid movement by large bodies of troops. For much the same reason the Germans were intent on denying rail lines to the Soviets and utilizing them for themselves (something that wasn't straightforward as European and Soviet railways operated different gauges) with converted or captured Russian stock. (From the fonds of the RGAKFD in Krasnogorsk via Stavka)

A *Kradschütze* serving with *Großdeutschland* poses, his gas-mask canister slung across his chest as was the fashion with motorcycle troops. Note the cuff title on the right sleeve: Infanterie-Regiment (mot.) – later Infanterie-Division (mot.) – *Großdeutschland* went through at least four versions of their cuff bands, the first two of gothic-style script, with this being the third (and least legible) example, a Sütterlin-style script introduced in September 1940 and lasting until mid-1944, when it was supplanted by the final iteration of the cuff band, a copperplate-style script. Originally founded as Wachregiment Berlin in 1921, the regiment was a ceremonial unit until the start of 1939, when it became Infanterie-Regiment *Großdeutschland*, a formation that drew its volunteer-only recruits from all over Germany. The regiment missed out on the Polish campaign as it was still in the process of being trained and motorized, but it served both in France and in the Balkan invasion that had immediately preceded *Barbarossa*. (Nik Cornish at www.stavka.org.uk)

open the German 'pincers' east of Smolensk. These groups – Group Maslennikov (29th Army) and Group Khomenko (30th Army) north of Iartsevo and Group Kalinin (24th Army) and Group Kachalov (28th Army) to the south – were to bite into the flanks of Heeresgruppe Mitte's encircling pincers, cutting them off and thus at the same time relieving the three beleaguered armies at Smolensk. Lieutenant-General Vladimir Y. Kachalov was ordered by Zhukov to 'concentrate in the … Roslavl region [110km south-south-east of Smolensk] by day's end 21 July and attack northward towards Smolensk on 22 July' (quoted in Glantz 2010: 196). The orders for Group Kachalov to attack on the 22nd (probably at 2200hrs) were pushed to 0400hrs on the morning of 23 July, and directed Kachalov, he recalled, 'to destroy opposing enemy forces, advance towards Smolensk into the rear of the enemy's El'nia grouping, reach the Strigino, Pochinok, and Trutnevo line [55km south-east to 52km south of Smolensk] by day's end on 23 July, and, subsequently, attack towards Smolensk' (quoted in Glantz 2010: 201).

Group Kachalov consisted of Major-General Fedor D. Zakharov's 149th Rifle Division, Major-General Alexander A. Volkhin's 145th Rifle Division, Colonel Vasily G. Burkov's 104th Tank Division and other elements including the 32nd Motorized Rifle Regiment, the 643rd and 364th Corps Artillery regiments, the 209th Assault Aviation Regiment and the 239th Fighter Aviation Regiment. Zakharov's 149th Rifle Division (479th, 568th and 744th Rifle regiments) was ordered to take the Chernavka–Voroshilovo–Likhnovo line (25km south-east of Pochinok) by first light on 23 July, then seize crossings over the Khmara River and move on to take Pochinok. Volkhin's 145th Rifle Division (403rd, 599th and 729th Rifle regiments, with the 340th Rifle Regiment of 46th Rifle Division attached) was expected to drive up the Roslavl–Smolensk road, forcing the enemy from the Stomet River line and taking Vas'kovo station, 17km south of Pochinok.

A reasonably strong force on paper, Group Kachalov (along with the other three groups) had severe underlying problems that would cost them dearly in the coming days; the armies were new and they were untrained and underequipped. 'Hastily organised literally overnight, these new rifle and tank divisions consisted primarily of partially-trained reservists and largely untrained conscripts strengthened by a cadre of NKVD officers and a leavening of former border guards' (Glantz 2010: 196-97). Lieutenant-General Andrei I. Eremenko, a senior commander of the Western Front, noted that the various elements of 28th Army were assembled at great haste from all over the Soviet Union; they only arrived in theatre on 10 July and had no time to conduct any sort of training, from platoon tactics on up through to regimental and divisional manoeuvres. There were shortages of heavy weapons as well as of ammunition, vehicles, engineering equipment and general supplies. There was no understanding – let alone experience – of working in combined-arms operations, and a callowness at almost every level of command excepting Kachalov's (who was a career soldier, serving since 1911).

These mostly untrained, untested, underequipped and inexperienced men were expected to move from a standing start into a pitched battle against a highly trained, experienced, well-equipped enemy, overcome him in short order, and push on towards Pochinok and then Smolensk.

That immediate enemy, at least for some of the regiments of 145th and 149th Rifle divisions, was to be Infanterie-Regiment (mot.) *Großdeutschland* (hereafter simply *Großdeutschland* or IR GD). The regiment consisted of 20 *Kompanien*, including *Panzerjäger*, *leichtes* and *schweres Infanterie-Geschütz*, *Sturmgeschütz* (assault gun), *Aufklärung* (reconnaissance), *Pionier* (combat engineer), *Nachrichten* (signals) and *Flak* (anti-aircraft) companies across five *Bataillonen*, as well as an additional artillery battalion, ArtAbt 400; all were motorized. Crossing the frontier at the Bug River on the night of 27/28 June, the well-rested and fully manned unit pushed along the 'R2' highway as part of General der Panzertruppen Heinrich von Vietinghoff's XXXXVI. Armeekorps (mot.), which also included 10. Panzer-Division and SS-Infanterie-Division (mot.) *Reich*. The regiment quickly understood that this was a different campaign from those in which it had previously fought. Attacks happened often and usually came out the blue, and could take the form of a single sniper or a vicious mêlée such as that at the village of Kamienka on 5–6 July. The constant vigilance and uncertainty was wearing: 'This situation of constant tension strained the nerves of the men to the breaking point. The resulting overexertion left the men somewhat indifferent, one could also say resigned, accepting everything as it came. This also explains the losses among officers and NCOs, which were dreadfully high at the outset of the campaign' (Spaeter 1992: 192).

Crossing the Dnieper under the aegis of 10. Panzer-Division on 11 July, *Großdeutschland* pushed forwards to Gorky and into the area south of Smolensk on 21 July, its orders 'to keep open the advance road of 10th Pz-Div, which was fighting farther ahead, and at the same time hold the major Smolensk–Roslavl road … [As well as] guarding the airfield near Motschuly' (Spaeter 1992: 203). *Großdeutschland* would spend the next five days trying desperately to follow those orders.

Großdeutschland SdKfz 250 half-tracks from 17. (Aufklärungs-Abteilung) Kompanie crossing the Russian steppe. The white helmet insignia of the regiment is clearly visible next to the unit marking (which is for a motorcycle reconnaissance unit – 17. Kompanie had one armoured-car and two motorcycle platoons). The main car in the picture is an SdKfz 250/10 reconnaissance platoon-leader's variant, produced 1940–43 and armed with a 3.7cm PaK 35/36 (the same underpowered gun that was used as a towed anti-tank piece). (Nik Cornish at www.stavka.org.uk)

Infanterie-Regiment (mot.) *Großdeutschland* and 729th Rifle Regiment at Vas'kovo–Voroshilovo, 23–27 July 1941

1 **0400hrs, 23 July:** At Vas'kovo, the 729th and 599th Rifle regiments of 145th Rifle Division move up the Pochinok–Roslavl road, crossing the Stomet River; after a fierce Soviet bombardment, the RKKA regiments attack I./IR GD's defensive positions on the northern bank of the Stomet, and are beaten back by concentrated machine-gun fire as well as fire from a pair of infantry guns. The unsuccessful Soviet attacks continue until nightfall.

2 **0530hrs–1530hrs, 23 July:** At Voroshilovo, 149th Rifle Division's 568th Rifle Regiment moves up through the village of Guta and attacks II./IR GD's line at Voroshilovo, but the assault is broken up by artillery and machine-gun fire. A later attack by 479th Rifle Regiment (also of 149th Rifle Division) from the south-east suffers the same fate. Repeated Soviet artillery bombardments and infantry attacks continue throughout the day, with a major assault by massed Soviet infantry launched at 1530hrs, but the attack is cut down once again, 200m shy of II./IR GD's line.

3 **0400hrs, 24 July:** At Vas'kovo, Soviet attacks recommence, but are broken up on the Stomet, in part by attacks from Ju 87 'Stuka' dive-bombers. At 0900hrs (approx.) the 599th Rifle Regiment attempts a flanking manoeuvre to the east; despite some temporary success it is beaten back with heavy losses by *Großdeutschland* reserves.

4 **0900hrs, 24 July:** At Voroshilovo, after a night of heavy shelling another massed Soviet infantry attack is launched by the 568th and 479th Rifle regiments, only to fail once again.

5 **1630hrs, 24 July:** At Voroshilovo, another punishing attack by 568th and 479th Rifle regiments finally bears fruit, as II./IR GD is forced to abandon its forward defensive line. By 1830hrs concerted German counter-attacks reinforced with Panzers push the Soviets back from their hard-won ground and stabilize the situation.

6 **1200hrs (approx.), 25 July:** At Vas'kovo, constant Soviet pressure from the 403th Rifle Regiment to the west, the 729th Rifle Regiment to the south and the 599th Rifle Regiment to the east begins to tell, forcing I./IR GD to pull back to a secondary line.

7 **0600hrs (approx.), 26 July:** The 403rd Rifle Regiment reaches Dmitriyevka, 11km behind I./IR GD's right flank.

8 **0800hrs, 26 July:** Elements of 149th Rifle Division reach Nikulino, outflanking II./IR GD's position to the east.

9 **26–27 July:** Overnight, I./IR GD is relieved and pulls out of Vas'kovo, quickly followed by II./IR GD at Voroshilovo. On 28 July Group Kachalov's attacks will force a 5km German withdrawal to a more defensible line, but fail to achieve any of their tactical objectives, with none of the 28th Army units even reaching the Khmara River line, the target for the first day of the attack.

Battlefield environment

The main strategic feature of the landscape was the railway line, running from Smolensk in the north-west to the south-east, though Pochinok and on to Roslavl, a distance of about 110km. The Smolensk–Roslavl road ran more or less parallel to a train line. Around 1km shy of the Stomet River there was a level crossing with a drainage pipe below that served as the headquarters for I./IR GD.

The environment was a mixture of woods, scrubland and sandy soil, interspersed with wheat fields and bisected by meandering, swampy rivers such as the Stomet. There were numerous small villages scattered throughout the area, of which Vas'kovo and Voroshilovo were two of the more significant. Both were to the north of the Stomet, with Voroshilovo about 7km to the east of Vas'kovo.

A Luftwaffe reconnaissance photo) showing the village of Vas'kovo. The Smolensk–Roslavl railway line runs through the centre of the picture (Pochinok lies 14km north-north-west of Vas'kovo and Smolensk 55km away), with the Smolensk–Roslavl road angling in from the west. The road and rail lines meet 3km south of the photo at the level crossing, near which was a drainage pipe that served as I./IR GD's command post during the battle. (John Calvin, wwii-photos-maps.com)

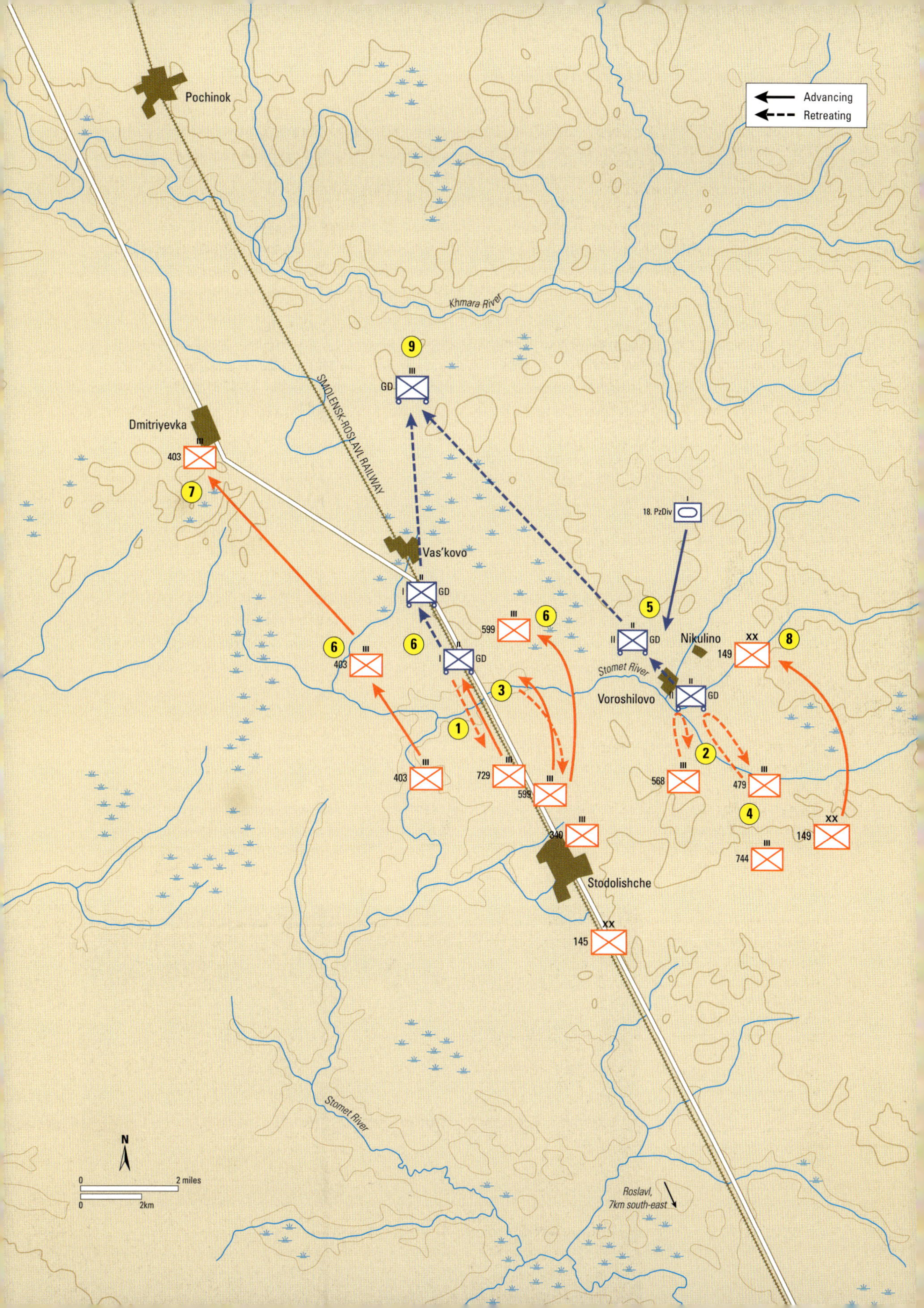
Advancing
Retreating
Pochinok
Khmara River
SMOLENSK–ROSLAVL RAILWAY
Dmitriyevka
403
GD
18. PzDiv
Vas'kovo
GD
599
403
GD
Nikulino
149
Stomet River
Voroshilovo
GD
GD
403
729
599
568
479
340
744
149
Stodolishche
145
Stomet River
Roslavl,
7km south-east
N
2 miles
2km

INTO COMBAT

The men of *Großdeutschland* took up defensive positions facing south and east; 2. and 3. Kompanien of I./IR GD, supported by Oberleutnant Karl Hänert's 4. (sMG) Kompanie and a pair of light infantry guns, positioned themselves around the level crossing at Vas'kovo (which they turned into the line's strongpoint, with the command post hidden in a drainage ditch beneath the road). Meanwhile, 5., 6. and 7. Kompanien of II./IR GD, together with 10. Kompanie of III./IR GD and 18. (Pionier) Kompanie, set up at Voroshilovo, with 7. Kompanie to the left, 5. Kompanie to the right and 6. Kompanie in reserve. The relative paucity of troops available, coupled with the size of the areas they had to defend, led to a front that was more widely spaced than was ideal: a report compiled by I./IR GD noted how 'On our right there are none of our own troops for 50 kilometres. On the left it is 20 kilometres to II Battalion' (quoted in Spaeter 1992: 204). The actual distance between I./IR GD at Vas'kovo and II./IR GD at Voroshilovo was closer to 7km, but the sense of isolation such widely staggered outposts fostered was very real.

The men of *Großdeutschland* knew that there were RKKA troops in the area, some as close as 6–7km south, though they were unaware that the fresh regiments of 145th Rifle Division were moving up the Smolensk–Roslavl road in preparation for an all-out attack. The sporadic artillery shelling that the men had been enduring for the last day or so suddenly increased in intensity as the dawn approached on the morning of 23 July; a member of I./IR GD noted that 'From 01.00 to 03.00 the fire was weaker. Then it thundered down with renewed vigour on the level crossing' (quoted in Spaeter 1992: 205). The observer noted how there was a pause in the artillery fire, and then:

> ... for a moment, we had a clear view [of] the field before us. – They're coming!! – Great masses of men were climbing down into the bottom land. Mounted officers circled round them. Everything ahead of us was brown with Russians ... Most of them were now in the bottom land. The Russian artillery fire ceased. Our ears were ringing ... Oblt. Hänert, commander of the machine gun company, stood in his slit trench. – 800 metres – He did nothing ... A sustained fire opened up from twelve machine guns at once. It began and ended abruptly ... In seconds the mass of men was gone. (Quoted in Spaeter 1992: 205)

RKKA infantry advance across open ground in a standard skirmish-line attack. The vulnerability of the attacking infantry was ideally mitigated by support from platoon- and company-level heavy weapons (such as the Maxim position shown on the right) as well as artillery, but severe shortages, inadequate training and in some cases an almost non-existent understanding of combined-arms tactics meant that the riflemen of the skirmish line were often exposed to essentially unchecked enemy fire. Casualties from such operations were as horrendous as the tactics were unsuccessful; however frightening it was for the German defenders to receive such brazen assaults, as long as their nerve held and their ammunition lasted, the outcome was usually obvious. (Courtesy of the Central Museum of the Armed Forces, Moscow via Stavka)

After another pause, the Soviet attackers began to reappear and return fire: 'The Russians ahead of us were about fifty metres away, firing without pause … For hours they came no farther. Had the attack been beaten off? The enemy artillery opened up again and the fire lasted into the night. Most of the Russians in front of us lay without cover. Many died screaming under their own fire' (quoted in Spaeter 1992: 206).

Major-General Alexander Volkhin's 145th Rifle Division had suffered greatly for little gain; the logistics of getting the men in position to attack had been painfully difficult, with some elements of the division marching up to 40km on 22 July just to get to the line. Once the frontal attacks of 729th and 599th Rifle regiments commenced they were met with stubborn and effective defence. Probably the best chance of the day's attacks on Vas'kovo had been a flank assault; Volkhin had directed the commander of one of the regiments of the division with an artillery battalion to make a flanking manoeuvre and attack the enemy in flank and rear. The regiment under the leadership of the commander of the 1st Battalion [403rd Rifle Regiment], Major Emelyanov, initially had success and continued for 3–4 km. The enemy threw in their reserves and superior forces ousted the regiment. (Eremenko 1965: 259)

With that failure Volkhin's regiments were more or less where they were when the day began. With the slackening of Soviet artillery fire at about 0100hrs the men of *Großdeutschland* began the task of collecting the wounded and the dead. All those killed had died from head or chest wounds, caused as they stood firing at the enemy. The Soviets mostly lay where they fell, out of reach of help.

At Voroshilovo the men of II./IR GD could hear the sounds of combat echo across from Vas'kovo in the early-morning air. Soon enough the men of 7. Kompanie saw movement to their own front as elements of 149th Rifle Division's 568th Rifle Regiment moved up through the small village of Guta, 700–800m to the south-south-east, which they fought off with infantry guns and artillery, followed soon after by a further attack from the south-east (probably carried out by the 479th Rifle Regiment) that was spotted early and fended off. Nevertheless the Soviets continued to probe the line, manoeuvring more troops and artillery into the area and starting to press an artillery attack at about 0900hrs against the position's right flank, held by Oberleutnant René de l'Homme de Courbière's 6. Kompanie. Further attacks came in from the east at about the same time but were broken up by fire from the light infantry guns and ArtAbt 400's 3. Batterie (four 15cm howitzers), all of which were now running short of ammunition. Another attack on 7. Kompanie got to

An excellent shot of a *Großdeutschland* 8cm GrW 34 and crew preparing for action. As was the practice for all motorized infantry, the fourth company of each of *Großdeutschland's* three rifle battalions was equipped with 12 HMGs and six GrW 34 mortars. Crewed by three men, weighing 56.7kg and firing a 3.5kg shell, the mortar could lay down up to 14 rounds per minute out to a maximum range of 2,200m (though 400–1,500m was optimal), and was the standard German medium mortar of the war. Due to the qualities of the weapon as well as the high level of training given to the crews the GrW 34 developed a reputation for pinpoint accuracy, which, coupled with its rapid rate of fire, made it a potent close-support weapon. (Nik Cornish at www.stavka.org.uk)

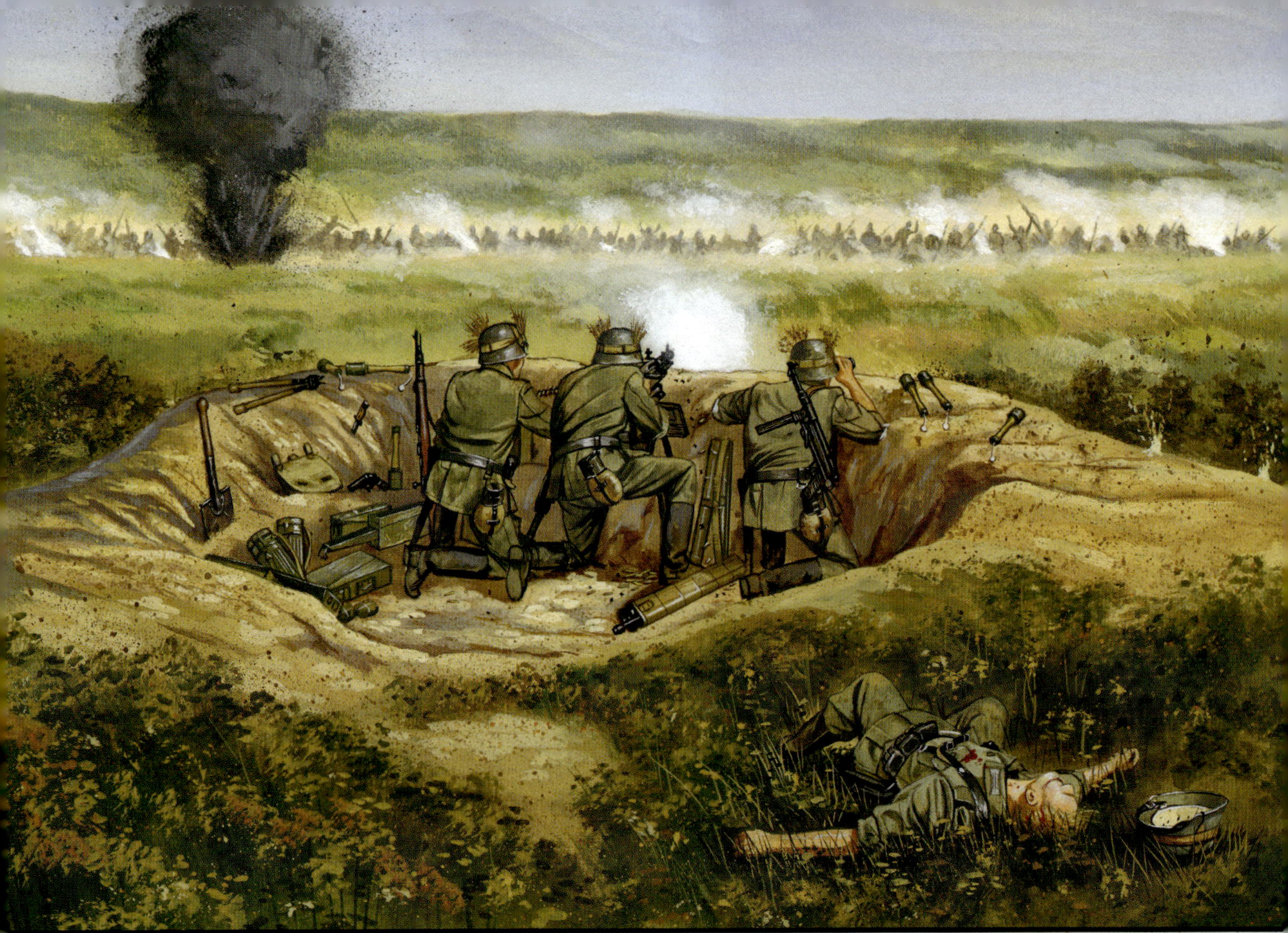

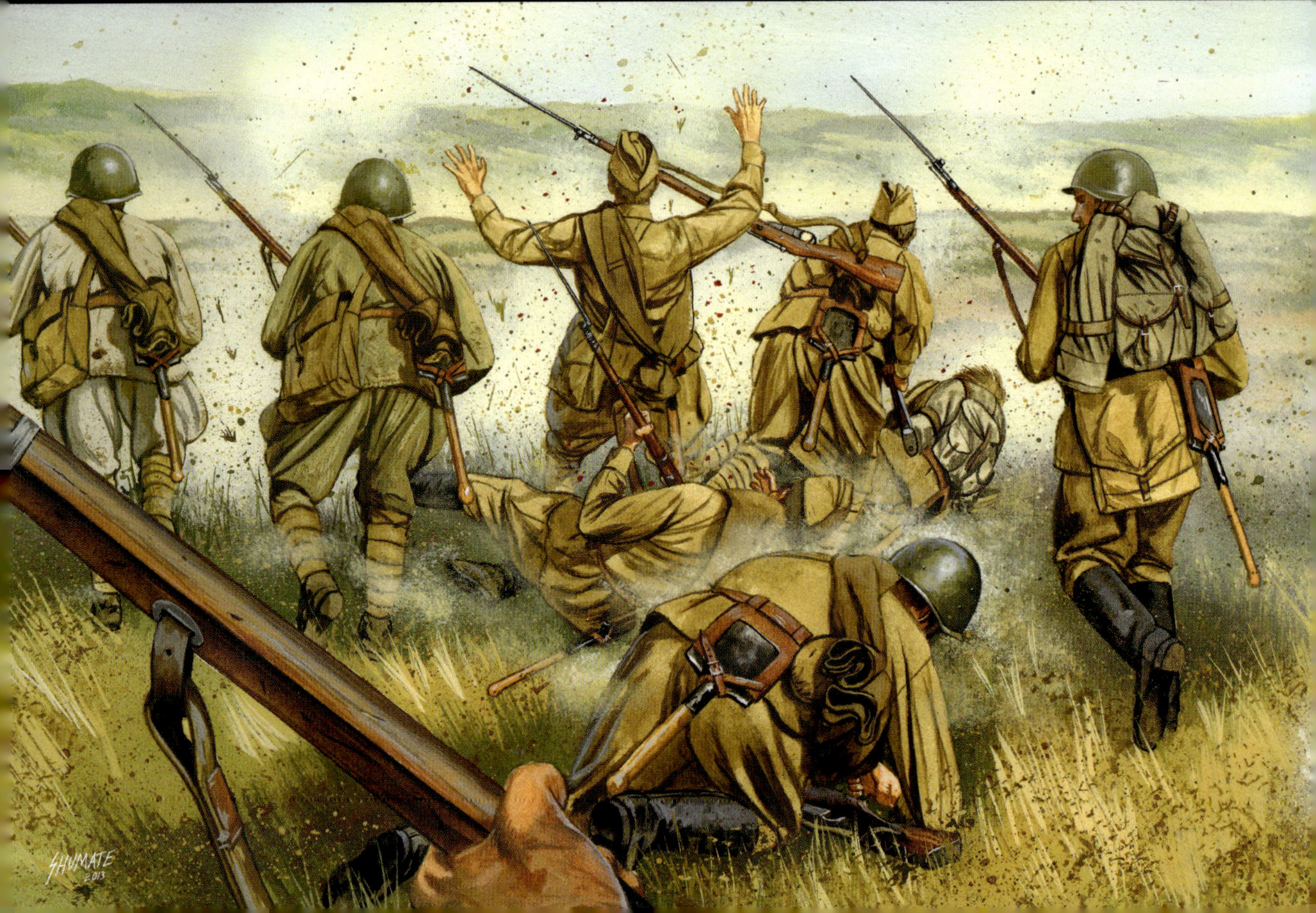
SHUMATE

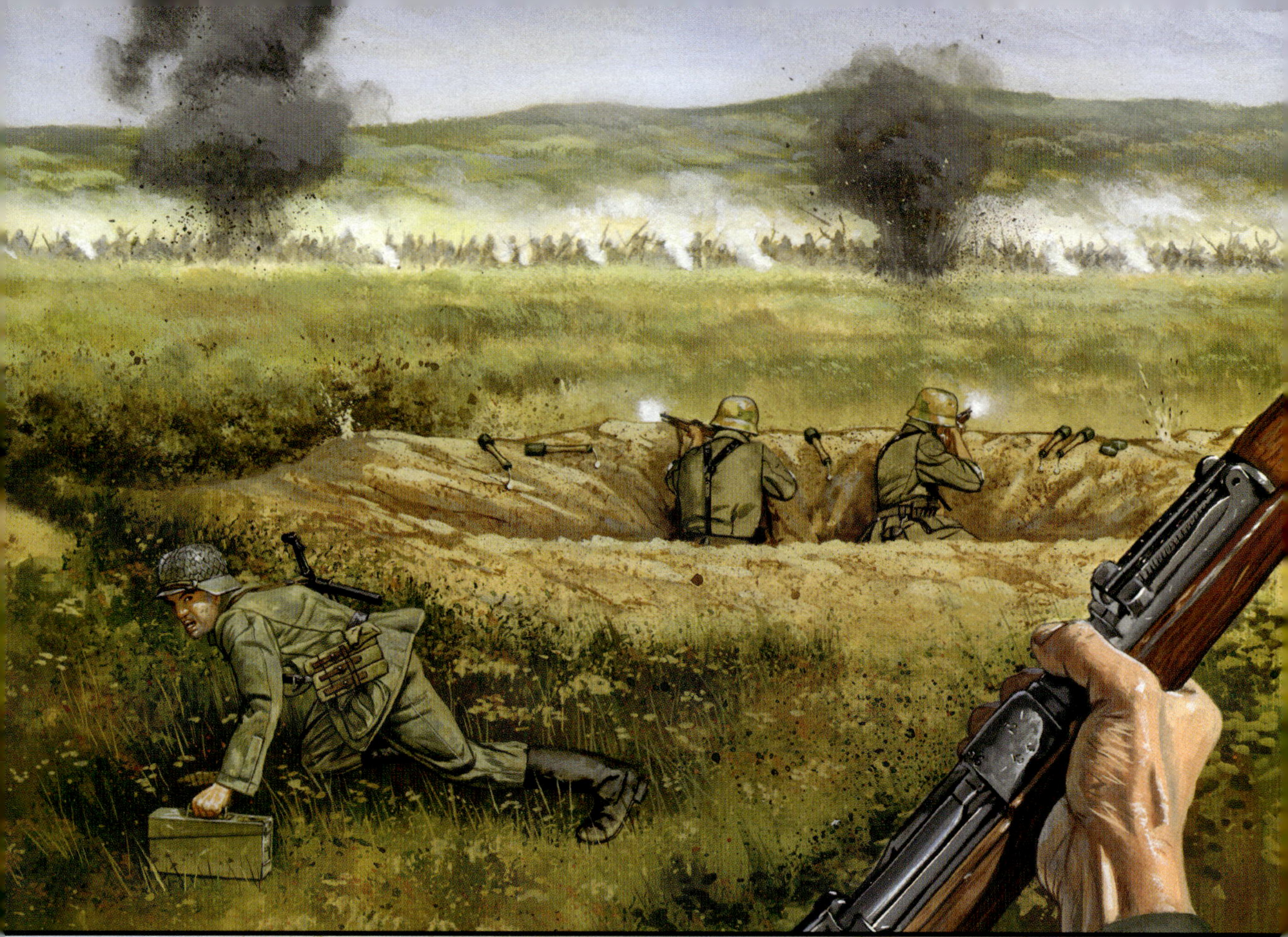

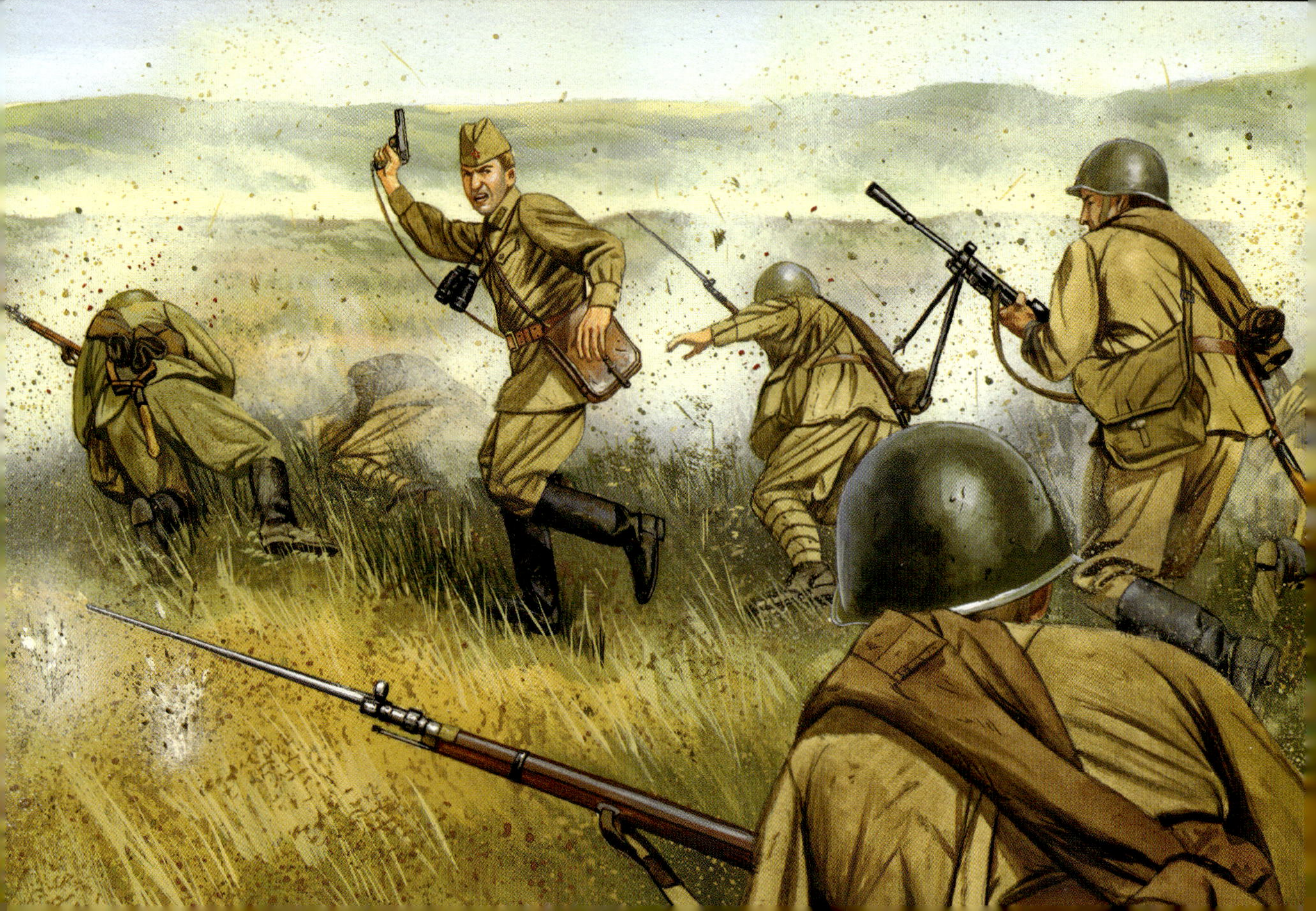

PREVIOUS PAGES

Clash at Vas'kovo

German view: Elements of I./IR GD have occupied the main road/railway line running from Smolensk to Roslavl. The Russians, after massive artillery assaults, are streaming out from the forest on the south of the river, moving across the shallow stream and up to the German positions in wave after disorderly wave, a great mass of men not slowed at all by the sporadic detonations of shells from a pair of *Großdeutschland*'s light infantry guns. The men of 1. Zug, 2. Kompanie, I./IR GD are strung out in a ragged line of two-man *Schützenloch* 'firing holes', roughly 10m apart, in a shallow semi-circle; the German position is strengthened by the 12 HMGs of Oberleutnant Karl Hänert's 4. (sMG) Kompanie that punctuate and back up the infantry's line. Waiting until the Russian attack closes to 200–400m, the whole German force unleashes its fire at brutally close range. An *Unteroffizier* crawls towards the HMG position with a *Patronenkasten* (containing 300 rounds of ammunition) while the gunners and nearby riflemen keep up a constant fire on the wall of Soviets surging towards them. The sMG (*schweres Maschinengewehr*, or 'heavy machine gun'), an MG 34 mounted on a Lafette 34 tripod, has extra barrels at the ready in a Laufschützer 34 ('barrel cover/guard', holding one spare barrel) and a Laufbehälter 34 ('barrel container', holding two spare barrels) to cope with the rapid heating that occurs during sustained fire.

Soviet view: The men of 145th Rifle Division, tasked with storming the Stomet River line and seizing the level crossing just south of Vas'kovo, are attacking up the main Roslavl–Smolensk road. Russian battalions, including a number from the 729th and 599th Rifle regiments, are massed into assault line after assault line, and charge forward en masse hard on the heels of a heavy artillery barrage. The German positions are almost invisible, they are so well dug in; the Soviet riflemen make good progress at first, crossing through marshy scrub that serves as the banks of the Stomet River and are charging towards the German left, but are cut to pieces by the concentrated force of over a dozen MG 34s as they come within reach of their goal. The men mostly wear summer uniforms of various shades with a mix of puttees and boots, and SSch-40 helmets as per regulations, though some still wear the ever-popular M-35 *pilotka* soft caps despite repeated instructions not to. Their officer waves his TT-33 semi-automatic pistol in the air, exhorting his rapidly disintegrating line of men to carry on, but cohesion evaporates as soldiers dive for cover or are cut down where they stand, the whole attack descending into a confusion of bodies, panic, dust and blood. Having no proper training in infantry tactics, unaware of how best to use the terrain to their advantage, and having no notable support from other arms or heavy weapons, the officers and men of the 729th and 599th Rifle Regiments instead rely on courage to carry the day. It is not enough.

within 300m before it was cut down by rifle and machine-gun fire supported by one or two 2cm FlaK guns. Though the attacks slackened there wasn't much respite; snipers in the trees caused the first German casualties, while the defenders suffered from the heat of the day and a lack of water, resupply having been interrupted.

The Soviet artillery started up again at 1430hrs and the third attack of the day began an hour later, a massed assault that stuttered to a halt under the fire of the defender's light and heavy machine guns, leaving the Russians 'bogged down 200 metres in front of the main line of resistance' (Spaeter 1992: 209) and with little option but to pull back as darkness fell. 10. Kompanie of III./IR GD was brought up to reinforce the line together with rations and ammunition, while the fighting positions were repaired and extended.

Kachalov, hearing that his divisions had been attacking all day and yet had barely moved from their starting positions, was incandescent. Raging against the failures he saw in his troops, he spat out a list of their inadequacies, including: the 'completely inadequate tempo of advance' of 145th and 149th Rifle divisions; a 'lack of audacity' at all levels of leadership; reliance on 'futile frontal attacks'; failure to exploit the terrain for envelopment; the pursuit of retreating enemy units 'on all fours'; poor use of infantry firepower; badly timed and inaccurate artillery support; and dismal reconnaissance (quoted in Glantz 2010: 204). 145th and 149th Rifle divisions were ordered to recommence their attacks at 0400hrs on 24 July.

At Vas'kovo Leutnant Maximilian Fabich's 3. Kompanie was brought forward from reserve and used to bolster the left wing. The attack was observed by Oberleutnant Rössert, commander of 2. Kompanie, who was fully aware of the value that effective aerial support lent to his men's position:

> The enemy reached the stream … [and] began to construct rafts and watercraft for a crossing. Thanks to the outstanding support from our Stukas, which had meanwhile appeared on the scene and with which we had very good communications through visual signals, the crossing attempt was, in the main, frustrated. The Stukas rained destruction on the Russians barely fifty metres ahead of our positions. Often, rafts with 30 to 40 Russians were hit and sunk … The only reply from the other side was furious machine gun fire which met the Stukas as they approached. (Quoted in Spaeter 1992: 210)

The Russians were in full agreement with Rössert, the fuming Colonel Ivan F. Dremov, commander of the 729th Rifle Regiment, noting how frustrating it was to have his regiment at the mercy of German aircraft that operated with 'impunity' against his men, 'thick as locusts, hanging in the sky, dropping hundreds of bombs onto the division's battle formations' (Dremov 1981), which did indeed lack almost all forms of anti-aircraft defence.

Volkhin tried to turn I./IR GD's flank once again, this time with the 599th Rifle Regiment: 'The next day [24 July], the solution of a flank attack was repeated with Major Korablinov's Regiment, but they failed. The combat capabilities of the division were down significantly due to large losses in personnel.

The Ju 87 'Stuka' (*Sturzkampfflugzeug*, or 'dive-bomber') was one of the defining machines of the Blitzkrieg era. The ability of German units to summon reliable, timely support was an often-critical advantage in the course of a fight: 'Called in by radio directly from the frontline commanders, dive-bombers or ground-attack aircraft would strike rapidly and hard against any encountered enemy stronghold … While close-support air units were in constant action over the front line, the task of the twin-engine tactical medium bombers was to destroy communication lines, headquarters, and airfields in the enemy's rear area' (Bergström & Mikhailov 2000: 6). Demand, however, always outstripped supply, as General der Flieger Wolfram von Richthofen noted: 'The Army refused to realise that the Luftwaffe could not be dribbled out at all places but must be concentrated at major points' (Bergström & Mikhailov 2000: 84). The toll on the opposing air forces, much as for the ground-combat units, was constant and severe. From 22 June to 31 July the VVS went from nearly 10,000 combat aircraft to fewer than 1,900 serviceable planes, while for the Luftwaffe the losses in roughly the same period came to 1,284 aircraft damaged or destroyed from the 3,000 that had started the campaign. (Cody Images)

67

Oberleutnant Rössert, Infanterie-Regiment (mot.) *Großdeutschland*

The soldiers of 2. Kompanie, I./IR GD relied absolutely upon their commander, Oberleutnant Rössert, during the grim and impossibly tense days dug into the dirt at Vas'kovo. He led them through four days of resolute defence during which the men looked to his calm demeanour to quell their own fears.

Having started his career in the Wachregiment Berlin, Rössert had moved with the majority of its personnel into the new Infanterie-Regiment *Großdeutschland*, taking up his place as a *Leutnant* in 8. Kompanie. He was soon hand-picked to run 2. Zug of the *Führer-Begleit-Kommando*, a personal escort and honour-guard for Adolf Hitler, during the Polish campaign. In April 1940 he moved back to *Großdeutschland* and – made up to *Oberleutnant* – took command of 2. Kompanie, I./IR GD, with which he campaigned through France. He was involved in planning the assault on Gibraltar (Operation *Felix*, never carried out) and then took part in the Axis campaign in the Balkans, where he led his *Kompanie* down to the Danube and then across into the burning city of Belgrade just as Easter morning broke.

Rössert was in many ways the ideal of a young German officer (certainly of a *Großdeutschland* officer), mixing flawless ceremonial duties with a bit of dashing adventure, all leavened with hard fighting and personal courage in combat. Perhaps surprisingly, considering what happened to most other young officers who shared his verve, Rössert would survive the war.

A Sturmgeschütz Ausf A or B armed with the short 7.5cm L/24. Assault guns were first and foremost an infantry-support weapon, meant to strengthen attacks and defeat strongpoints as well as counter the threat of enemy armour. IV./IR GD's 16. Kompanie had one battery of six StuG; these found themselves parcelled out along the Vas'kovo–Voroshilovo line, supplementing the infantry guns in their defensive support of the hard-pressed infantry. (Nik Cornish at www.stavka.org.uk)

The attack had to continue, despite the heavy losses, because of the situation prevailing in Smolensk and in El'nia' (Eremenko 1965: 259). The difficulties they were having certainly made the Soviet commanders assume that they were up against more significant forces than those that actually faced them, with Volkhin stating (in the hyperbolic way that seemed to come so easily to RKKA commanders) that he was dealing with an enemy that had four times his own strength.

The Soviet artillery may not have always worked well in co-ordination with the attacking infantry, but it still caused damage. When the Soviet guns were in full flow the men of *Großdeutschland* could do almost nothing, as noted in a situation report from I./IR GD: 'While under artillery fire there are only three possibilities: either one is not hit at all, or one is temporarily buried alive, or there is a direct hit. Then it's all over in any case. In artillery fire one must remain in one place. Many have died while searching for a better place' (quoted in Spaeter 1992: 204). The frequency and intensity of the bombardments was starting to tell, with many of I./IR GD's heavy weapons and wireless communications knocked out. Stoppages among most of the

> ## Lieutenant-Colonel Ivan Dremov, 729th Rifle Regiment
>
> In his way, Ivan Fyodorovich Dremov typified a type of ambitious career officer who served in the Great Patriotic War, as the Soviets called the 1941–45 conflict. Born in 1901 in the small village of Iskovka in Samara province, he would come of age in one of his country's most febrile periods. Joining the Red Army in 1919, he did well out of the Civil War, using it to get into the 3rd Infantry School in Smolensk, where the atmosphere was hard but optimistic. Graduating with a commission, he served as a junior infantry officer before going on to Moscow's Frunze Military Academy (the RKKA's Staff College, tasked with preparing officers for higher command, was renamed in honour of Mikhail Frunze, the academy's leader in 1923–25). Dremov had talent and worked his way up steadily, gaining some more experience in the Finnish campaign before he was given command of the 729th Rifle Regiment in the summer of 1940.
>
> The outbreak of war was a boon for an ambitious, aggressive man like Dremov; he fought his regiment hard, showing plenty of personal courage, but he also knew how to survive in the dangerously political world of the senior army commanders. Escaping the destruction of the 28th Army, Dremov stepped from the ruins of his rifle regiment to the command of a mechanized brigade in 1942, and from there eventually rising to command 8th Guards Mechanized Corps, ending the war a major-general and a Hero of the Soviet Union. He retired in 1958 and died on 2 September 1983, aged 82.

machine guns due to dirt and sand exacerbated the problem, and soon small groups of Russians were slipping through and around the German defences, forcing Feldwebel Stadler's 1. Zug of 2. Kompanie to pull back after it was surrounded. The road to the rear of I./IR GD's position was briefly cut and only the commitment of men from 1. and 3. Kompanien, backed up by *Sturmgeschütze*, stabilized the situation.

Meanwhile at Voroshilovo Oberleutnant de Courbière's 6. Kompanie was the target for a redoubled Soviet offensive. Major-General Zakharov, commander of 149th Rifle Division, had ordered his divisional artillery commander, Colonel Pankov, to keep up a harassing fire throughout the night leading up to a massive bombardment – set for 0350hrs – that would precede the assault of his two rifle regiments (568th and 479th) at 0400hrs. For the defenders, it was a case of waiting, and watching, as reported by 6. Kompanie:

> Dust clouds behind and in front of the enemy lines indicated that still more guns were being moved forward … Our machine guns remained silent. We were not to open fire until the enemy had approached to point-blank range. The Russians approached ever nearer under cover of their artillery fire, pulling with them heavy machine guns on small two-wheeled carriages and hastily moving light artillery pieces into position … Finally, at 09.00, the enemy went to the attack, and once again his dense ranks were shot to pieces by our machine guns. (Quoted in Spaeter 1992: 211)

The German position was tenuous, with little in the way of heavy support and an ever-dwindling number of working machine guns to call upon. As the afternoon wore on the battalions of the 568th and 479th Rifle regiments recommenced the attack and by 1630hrs the positions of 6. Kompanie's leading *Zuge* were pierced and outflanked, forcing de Courbière to abandon the forward line. 'The last hand grenades were thrown at the enemy, then we left our holes … We dragged the wounded along with us … We had only four rifles left between us … The remnants of 6th Company assembled at the battalion command post – there were no more than seven men. Where were

OPPOSITE
A cluster of RGD-33 and RPG-40 hand grenades sit ready for use in this image from a slightly later period of the war. The RGD-33 (*Ruchnaya Granata Dyakonov*, or 'Dyakonov's hand grenade') could be thrown roughly 40m with an effective blast radius of 10m (increased to 15m if a fragmentation jacket was slipped over the explosive head), and together with the F1 'Limonka' (a 'lemon' shaped grenade with a 15m blast radius) provided the standard Soviet hand-grenade armament for the early part of the war. The explosive performance of the RGD-33 and the F1 was comparable with those of their German counterparts (the M24 'Potato Masher' and M39 'Egg' hand grenades), though the RGD-33 was overly complex to manufacture and had the rather fiddly requirement for the user to insert the fuse immediately before use. It was quickly supplanted by the far simpler RG-42 the following year, though the F1 continued in service throughout the war and well after, its design proving more robust. The two larger grenades are RPG-40s (*Ruchnaya Protivotankovaya Granata*, or 'hand-held tank grenade'), anti-tank weapons that were effective against lightly armoured vehicles and earlier-model Panzers (PzKpfw I–III), though as their lethal radius was more or less the same as their effective throwing distance (20–25m), their use required a certain amount of courage. (Courtesy of the Central Museum of the Armed Forces, Moscow via Stavka)

the others?' (quoted in Spaeter 1992: 212). Counter-attacks by 5. and 10. Kompanien, followed by 18. (Pionier) Kompanie, came to nothing, but armoured reinforcement from 18. Panzer-Division at 1830hrs helped to put things back on an even keel, at least for a while.

Kachalov's night was at least as frustrating as the one he had endured the day before. Once more his divisions had been fighting all day and yet had seen only very localized successes, and those (notably 149th Rifle Division's brief capture of Voroshilovo) had been almost instantly overturned. Once more Kachalov reiterated what he expected from his men, as well as his senior artillerists, whom he insisted should take their place at the front to personally ensure that the fire of their guns was not wasted on poorly plotted enemy positions. Orders were extremely detailed, as they had to state not just an objective, but the method by which it might be achieved – in effect, an attempt to teach some of his more gauche subordinates 'on the job'. Such efforts were obviously doomed, but there were no alternatives – the attacks had to be launched because Smolensk had to be relieved.

The next day brought no respite for either attacker or defender. For the Germans, casualties had become so numerous that it was impossible to hold an unbroken perimeter. Promised relief never came, and the men of I./IR GD were forced to try to hold on, as they later reported:

> Another day of the heaviest fighting went by until, finally, the Russians achieved penetrations in every company's sector. Following the assault the Russians shared holes with the dead Grenadiers. Germans and Russians were often only 20 metres apart. Here a slit trench with Grenadiers, next to it one with Russians and, as always, Russians in the bushes ahead. For hours the battle raged with rifles, hand grenades and pistols. In the long run our position was hopeless. In the evening we began to take fire from directly behind. (Quoted in Spaeter 1992: 216)

The perseverance of the Soviets seemed to be paying off from the German perspective, though the view from Kachalov's position was far more disappointing. By the morning of 25 July the 403rd Rifle Regiment had made some progress in flanking I./IR GD's position at Vas'kovo to the right, but took another whole day to get as far as Dmitriyevka, 11km behind the Vas'kovo level crossing. On the western axis elements of 149th Rifle Division had moved around II./IR GD's left flank to enter Nikulino by 0800hrs on the morning of 26 July, but had failed to dislodge the defenders at Voroshilovo.

For the Germans relief finally arrived in the shape of a machine-gun battalion that was to take over *Großdeutschland*'s positions: 'Silently the Grenadiers crept from their holes. The damaged guns and heavy weapons were brought back with the men as were the wounded ... A Russian patrol followed only 50 metres behind. It was driven off with hand grenades' (quoted in Spaeter 1992: 217). I./IR GD withdrew on the night of 26/27 July, with the men of II./IR GD at Voroshilovo hard on their heels.

For the Soviets, the casualties were as awful as one would expect; up to 28 July 145th Rifle Division lost 2,141 men and 149th Rifle Division lost 966 men. For Group Kachalov as a whole, the losses (up to 31 July) were 7,903 men, including 1,128 KIA and 1,570 missing (TsAMO RF, f. 208, Op. 2579, 22, I. 8). *Großdeutschland* had lost 455 men during 20–25 July.

For Kachalov's 28th Army, the following days would bring their effective annihilation as a fighting force, and for the men of *Großdeutschland* there would be more of what they had just gone through, almost without respite, for the rest of the year. Oberleutnant Karl Hänert, the commander of 4. (sMG) Kompanie, I./IR GD, who had done so much to secure the position at Vas'kovo, was awarded the Knight's Cross on 23 August 1941 for his conduct in the battle. He was killed at Briansk seven weeks later.

The problems suffered by *Großdeutschland* at Vas'kovo–Voroshilovo were common to the other motorized units of the *Panzergruppen*. As David Glantz has noted:

> Although all of these mobile divisions tried to economise forces by assigning their reconnaissance (motorcycle), engineer and other combat support battalions their own defensive sectors, their battalion frontages were far too wide to be effective either in defence or in attack. This, in turn, also caused inordinate casualties among the motorized infantry, which only exacerbated the problem of excessive frontages. (Glantz 2010: 249)

Being so far ahead of the rest of the army also caused the Germans problems with food, fuel and ammunition: 'The supply lines were already so far from the supply bases, and the supply roads so often interrupted by enemy incursions, that the ammunition simply could not be delivered' (Spaeter 1992: 210).

'General Kachalov's Army fought bravely and courageously, even though failure seemed to dog her every step' (Dremov 1981). In reality the task that Group Kachalov was given was nearly impossible, bearing in mind the nature of his rapidly assembled force. Soviet casualties were much higher than they should have been because basic tactics weren't understood or were misapplied, and the benefits of a well-supported combined-arms approach were non-existent: 'the ineffectiveness of Kachalov's forces, in particular their tendency to conduct costly frontal attacks and their inability to employ armor en masse and provide the infantry with adequate artillery support' (Glantz 2010: 308) meant that the thinly stretched German line held out. Nevertheless the relentless artillery bombardments and attacks that were thrown against *Großdeutschland* and the other defenders of the line came close enough to succeeding that Guderian made a point of turning on 28th Army and cutting it to pieces. The regiments and divisions were annihilated or escaped in such a reduced fashion as to be militarily worthless. Kachalov was killed while trying to lead a break out through Starinka on 4 August, though in the confusion of battle his fate wasn't known for many months, and he was assumed to be a traitor by the country he died defending.

Analysis

LESSONS LEARNED: THE GERMANS

For the Wehrmacht's motorized-infantry units Operation *Barbarossa* seemed to promise great things. The vast space of the steppes appeared to offer unparalleled opportunities for a force designed specifically for a war of manoeuvre, but there were only 80,000km of railways (for the Germans, of the wrong gauge), and 64,000km of hard-surfaced all-weather roads, most other roads being either dirt tracks or so poorly metalled by a single layer of gravel that the passage of a few vehicles was enough to start wearing the surface away. The dismal state of the roads became an immediate logistical problem as motorized formations discovered that they were using twice the amount of fuel usually allocated for the distance they were travelling (23,520 litres per day for a motorized regiment jumped to over 50,000 litres per day), with wear and tear on vehicles also more apparent, with frequent breakdowns of greater severity. Even so, the speed, tactical training and flexible, combined-arms approach of the German motorized and armoured spearheads made them fearsomely effective both in immediate tactical situations and also in larger strategic manoeuvres, where they far outstripped their Soviet opponents time and again. Despite such successes they were not well trained in defensive tactics, a notable gap considering the double defensive ring they were expected to maintain during the forming of a *Kessel*, and their lighter establishment of infantry compared to a standard German infantry division meant that losses cut deeper, faster.

Of course the armoured and motorized elements of the *Heeresgruppen* were only a small percentage of the overall forces employed, even if their speed and forward positions meant that they engaged in a disproportionate amount of fighting. The majority of the Heer's personnel walked to the battlefield, with equipment and artillery drawn by horses, not vehicles. This led to tactical problems whereby the motorized elements were often so far in advance of the infantry that they had to choose between stalling their advance, allowing the footsloggers to catch up, or pushing on and risking unsupported engagements with whatever RKKA unit they came across next. In most cases they pushed on, but the punishment this exacted on the vehicles coupled with the casualties incurred in almost daily fighting against a determined foe eroded the offensive capability of Panzer and motorized units.

For the motorized-infantry regiments at Zhlobin, Smolensk and Vas'kovo–Voroshilovo the strength and flexibility afforded by good leadership and sound offensive tactics would prove to offer diminishing returns as each encounter moved further away from a training 'ideal'. At Zhlobin there was no forward planning or effective reconnaissance, resulting in an initially messy encounter that, considering the size and aggression of the Soviet battle group, could have gone very poorly for the Germans. However, IR 41 adapted to the situation with great speed, outflanking their enemy and forcing him to retreat. For IR 15 at Smolensk the benefits of motorization fell flat once the regiment was in the city, where street-fighting was the order of the day, similar to *Großdeutschland* at Vas'kovo–Voroshilovo, where the defensive nature of their position allowed little in the way of clever manoeuvres, calling more for endurance than anything else.

Right from the outset the defiance of the Soviet soldier, even in the face of impossible odds, was noted by the Germans, with Generaloberst Halder noting on 24 June how 'the stubborn resistance of individual Russian units is remarkable' (quoted in Clark 1985: 56). More ominously for an army whose successes had been in part defined by the other side 'playing the game', to one senior German planner it appeared that 'The Russians simply do not recognise great operational successes and are not at all influenced by them' (Generalmajor Adolf Heusinger, quoted in Glantz 1997: 350). The Germans characterized their Soviet opponent as being brave on the one hand but also stolid and devoid of initiative on the other, perhaps in an attempt to explain the contradictory nature of a combatant who seemed to fight to the bitter end one moment and then surrender en masse the next. The document 'Peculiarities of Russian Warfare' written by German officers for the US Army after the war still maintained that 'the Russian soldier ... possesses neither the perception nor the ability to think independently. He is subject to moods which for us are incomprehensible; he acts instinctively. As a soldier, the Russian is primitive and unassuming, brave by virtue of natural inclination, but morosely vegetating in a group' (US Army 1949: 6–7). SS-Gruppenführer Max Simon had a more considered view: 'The reasons [for the German failure in the East] did not lie in terrain and space, nor to the opposition put up by the air force or the artillery, nor can mere numbers or weapons have been decisive factors. The ability of the Russian infantry who fanatically contested every foot of our advance was the principal, perhaps only, reason' (quoted in Lucas 1991: 53).

RKKA soldiers surrender as a BT-7 light tank burns in the background. The huge number of prisoners taken in the border battles and the *Kesselschlacht* of Bialystok–Minsk (which alone accounted for around 300,000 POWs) quickly became a major problem for the Germans, who were logistically unprepared for victories on such a scale. Such surprise does not excuse the treatment meted out to such unfortunates, which would extend to shooting the wounded or sick, forced labour, a deliberate policy of starvation, and, for tens of thousands of prisoners, execution at the hands of *Einsatzgruppen* or the SS on political or racial grounds. The notorious *Kommissarbefehl* ('Commissar Order') of March 1941, insisting that all Soviet political officers be shot out of hand, was compounded by the general attitude – reinforced by the exhortations of some senior officers – that the Soviet forces, due to their supposed racial inferiority, were not due the same consideration and rights as other combatants. This appalling behaviour would have long-term consequences, partly in the form of the partisan movement that had its origin in Soviet stragglers from the early encirclements trapped behind the rapidly advancing German lines. (Nik Cornish at www.stavka.org.uk)

Aftermath

A German soldier poses beside a road sign bearing a rather pointed message. The difficulties of the Wehrmacht's campaign were exacerbated by the 'foreignness' of the Soviet lands compared to those of France and the Low Countries: the vastness was unsettling, the great distances wearing on men and machines, the roads were almost universally awful, and the climate was by turns parchingly hot or horribly humid. The seemingly unknowable nature of their enemy completed the sense of alienation that many German soldiers felt in those first months of the campaign. (Nik Cornish at www.stavka.org.uk)

The fall of Smolensk at the end of July wasn't the end of the battle in that sector; it would rage on until 10 September, with further Soviet counter-attacks around El'nia in August forcing the Germans into their first limited retreat of the campaign. Lukin's 16th Army then made a partial escape from the Smolensk *Kessel*, but it was only a temporary reprieve for most of them – including 129th Rifle Division, which was annihilated in the battles at Vyazma in October. Guderian, in response to the threat that Kachalov's 28th Army had posed to his southern flank, turned and encircled it, destroying it almost completely in 48 hours (though some portions of 149th Rifle Division managed to escape the disaster and struggled on after absorbing what was left of 145th Rifle Division, eventually being disbanded at the end of the year). For the men of Panzergruppe 2, however, there was another fight on the immediate horizon, as on 6 August most of the force – eventually including *Großdeutschland*, 10. Infanterie-Division (mot.) and 29. Infanterie-Division (mot.) – began wheeling to the south to join the encirclement of Kiev (23 August–26 September).

German operational planning for *Barbarossa* had been extensive, but the Wehrmacht's logistical planning proved to be completely inadequate. Replacements and supplies were slow to come and the ceaseless advancing and fighting, with always another hill to cross or strongpoint to take, was beginning to exhaust the men who formed the tip of the Wehrmacht's armoured spear. These consequences, only just becoming apparent as the July battles around Smolensk raged on, would have an ever more serious impact in the coming months. These factors exposed larger problems for the Germans: the strategy for the campaign was not tightly focused on discernible objectives, instead looking to more generalized goals involving the destruction of the RKKA or the capture of local resources, leading to a 'conceptual disconnect between even the most decisive battlefield victories … and how they might serve to translate into a victorious war' (Citino 2011: 140). This lack of strategic focus, coupled with a short-term approach to supplying the needs of the nation's war machine – the German manufacturing base was still operating on a civilian model, and would continue to do so until Dr Albert Speer became Minister of Armaments in early 1942– wouldn't have mattered if the Soviets went the way of the French or the Poles, but they didn't. Generaloberst Halder, a man who in early July had believed the campaign to be more or less over, had been forced by the events of that month to re-evaluate his earlier confident stance when he noted on 11 August:

> The whole situation makes it increasingly plain that we have underestimated the Russian colossus ... [Soviet] divisions are not armed and equipped according to our standards, and their tactical leadership is often poor. But there they are, and if we smash a dozen of them, the Russians simply put up another dozen... They are near their own resources, while we are moving farther and farther away from ours. And so our troops, sprawled over an immense front line, without any depth, are subjected to the incessant attacks of the enemy. (Quoted in Glantz 2001: 85)

For the Soviet Union, the initial losses of men and machines were so great that a state of more or less constant emergency would exist right though until the massive counter-attacks of December 1941. The RKKA would reorganize in the face of these overwhelming problems, making a virtue of necessity by simplifying command structures and re-evaluating the tactics employed by men and mechanized forces. Most importantly, the Soviets bought themselves the time to do this by fighting at every opportunity, launching attacks and counter-attacks that slowed, then blunted the strength of their enemy. Tukhachevsky, that great Soviet general whom the purges claimed as their most significant military victim, had considered the consequences of a German attack on his homeland:

> As for the Blitzkrieg, which is so propagandised by the Germans, this is directed towards an enemy who doesn't want to and won't fight it out. If the Germans meet an opponent who stands up and fights and takes the offensive himself, that would give a different aspect to things. The struggle would be bitter and protracted; by its very nature it would induce great fluctuations in the front on this side or that side and in great depth. In the final resort, all would depend on who had the greater moral fibre and who was at the close of the operations disposed of operational reserves in depth. (Quoted in Erickson 1983: 5)

RKKA infantry scramble through the rubble of a ruined village, one of a countless number of small hamlets and towns that would be wrecked by the passage of the front line and the subsequent depredations of the rear-echelon troops that followed it. Note the fact that all three men wear the *Pilotka* rather than their helmets, and carry little more than their weapons. Such men faced the constant threat of punishment from one's own side, with NKVD squads shooting stragglers, and senior officers (such as the desperately unfortunate Pavlov and the unjustly maligned Kachalov) being executed or damned as traitors for failing to achieve the impossible. Powerlessness in the face of seemingly unstoppable German advances led the GKO into acts of panicked viciousness, punishing the officers and men for failings that were institutional. Such violence was often unwarranted and of dubious use. (Courtesy of the Central Museum of the Armed Forces, Moscow via Stavka)

UNIT ORGANIZATIONS

German motorized-infantry regiment

The standard *Infanterie-Regiment* contained 3,049 men – 75 officers, seven administrators, 493 NCOs and 2,474 enlisted men. It was made up of: a regimental headquarters. including *Pionier* (combat engineer), signals and motorcycle platoons; three *Infanterie-Bataillonen*; a 13. Infanteriegeschütz-Kompanie (infantry gun company – 180 all ranks), manning six 7.5cm leIG 18 guns and two 15cm sIG 33 guns; and a 14. Panzerjäger-Kompanie (anti-tank company – approx. 180 all ranks), manning 12 3.7cm PaK 36 guns or 5cm PaK 38 guns, plus four MG 34 LMGs. All troops were motorized, and each gun was towed by a dedicated prime mover (usually the SdKfz 10) or a 1-tonne truck.

An *Infanterie-Bataillon* (22 officers and 839 men) contained: a headquarters element (five officers, 27 men); a motorcycle messenger platoon (18 men); three *Schützenkompanien* (rifle companies, each of four officers and 187 men); and a *schwere Kompanie* (heavy company – five officers, 197 men) manning 12 *schwere* (heavy) MG 34 machine guns and six 8cm GrW 34 mortars. A *Schützenkompanie* contained a command element (one officer, 12 men) and three *Schützenzuge* (rifle platoons). A *Schützenzug* (one officer, 48 men), led by a *Leutnant* with a *Feldwebel* as his second in command, was made up of four ten-man *Schützengruppen* and a three-man section manning a 5cm GrW 36 mortar. The figures given here are for a standard *Infanterie-Regiment* from 1940–41, as the KStN tables (*Kriegsstärkenachweisungen*, or 'war strength lists') for specific motorized formations are unavailable. The motorized-infantry regiment (having the same organization and weaponry) differed very little in the essentials from its pedestrian counterpart. There would likely be some (small) variation in headquarters elements as well as ancillary units such as the regimental supply train.

In contrast, Infanterie-Regiment (mot.) *Großdeutschland* (as of 22 June 1941 with an estimated strength, including ArtAbt 400, of 6,050 all ranks – 151 officers and 5,899 men) fielded five organic battalions plus an additional artillery battalion, ArtAbt 400. Three of the regiment's battalions – I., II. and III. – each followed the standard structure set out above; IV. Bataillon grouped together 13. (LeIG) Kompanie, 14. (Panzerjäger) Kompanie, 15. (sIG) Kompanie and 16. (Sturmgeschütz) Kompanie, while V. Bataillon contained 17. (Aufklärungs) Kompanie, 18. (Pionier) Kompanie, 19. (Nachrichten) Kompanie and 20. (FlaK) Kompanie.

Soviet rifle regiment

The M-41 (April) Soviet rifle regiment contained 3,182 men – 131 officers, 56 political officers, 435 NCOs and 2,560 enlisted men. It was made up of: a headquarters element (15 officers, three political officers, four men); a supply department (seven officers, eight men); an HQ platoon (one officer, 27 men); a mounted reconnaissance platoon (one officer, 50 men); a signals company (four officers, one political officer, 73 men); an AA machine-gun company (three officers, one political officer and 46 men) with six PM (*Pulemyot Maxima*, or 'Maxim's machine gun') M1910 quad Maxim machine guns and three DShK 1938 12.7mm machine guns; a pioneer company (four officers, one political officer, 88 men); a chemical platoon (one officer, 19 men); three rifle battalions; a regimental gun battery (six officers, one political officer, 127 men) manning six 76mm M1927 guns; an anti-tank battery (four officers, one political officer, 51 men) manning six 45mm M1937 anti-tank guns; and a heavy-mortar battery (three officers, one political officer, 49 men) with four 82mm M37 mortars.

A rifle battalion (24 officers, four political officers, 636 men) contained: a headquarters element (four officers, one man); a signals platoon (one officer, 32 men); three rifle companies; and a machine-gun company (four officers, one political officer, 90 men) made up of a company HQ and three machine-gun platoons, (each with one officer and four MG squads, each squad comprising seven men and manning one DS-39 or PM M1910 machine gun). A rifle company (five officers, one political officer, 171 men) contained: a headquarters element (one officer, one political officer, five men); a five-man medical section; three rifle platoons; and a machine-gun platoon (one officer, 11 men). A rifle platoon (one officer, 50 men) contained a three-man command element (one officer, 2 men), four 11-man squads and a four-man mortar team with a 50mm RM-38, -39 or -40 mortar. Ancillary units added another 221 officers, NCOs and men to complete the regiment's establishment (transportation company, 107 men; medical company, 55 men; veterinary hospital, 12 men; workshops, 34 men; band, 13 men).

BIBLIOGRAPHY

Bergström, Christer & Mikhailov, Andrey (2000). *Black Cross Red Star: The Air War over the Eastern Front, Vol. 1 Operation Barbarossa, 1941.* Pacifica Military History.

Buchner, Alex (1991). *The German Infantry Handbook 1939–1945.* Atglen, PA: Schiffer.

Citino, Robert M. (2011). 'The Prussian Tradition, the Myth of the *Blitzkrieg* and the Illusion of German Military Dominance, 1939–41', in Frank McDonough (ed.), *The Origins of the Second World War: An International Perspective.* London: Continuum, pp. 126–43.

Clark, Alan (1985). *Barbarossa: The Russian-German Conflict, 1941–45.* London: Macmillan.

Cohen, Laurie R. (2013). *Smolensk Under the Nazis: Everyday Life in Occupied Russia.* Rochester, NY: University of Rochester Press.

Dremov, Ivan (1981). *Nastupala hroznaja bronia* ('Came the Formidable Armour'). Kiev: Publishing House of Political Literature of Ukraine. Available online at http://ta-1g.narod.ru/mem/dremov/dremov.html (accessed 5 February 2014).

Eremenko, Andrei (1965). *V nachale voyny* ('At the Beginning of the War'). Moscow: Nauka. Available online at http://militera.lib.ru/memo/russian/eremenko_ai_1/index.html (accessed 5 February 2014).

Erickson, John (1983). *Stalin's War with Germany. Vol. 1: The Road to Stalingrad.* London: Weidenfeld & Nicolson.

Fugate, Bryan (1988). *Operation Barbarossa: Strategy and Tactics on the Eastern Front, 1941.* Novato, CA: Presidio Press.

Glantz, David M., ed. (1997). *The Initial Period of War on the Eastern Front, 22 June–August 1941.* London: Frank Cass.

Glantz, David M. (2001). *Barbarossa: Hitler's Invasion of Russia 1941.* Stroud: Tempus.

Glantz, David M. (2005). *Companion to Colossus Reborn: Key Documents & Statistics*, Lawrence, KA: University Press of Kansas.

Glantz, David M. (2010). *Barbarossa Derailed: The Battle for Smolensk 10 July–10 September 1941 Vol. 1: The German Advance, The Encirclement Battle, and the First and Second Soviet Counteroffensives, 10 July–24 August 1941*, Solihull: Helion.

Guderian, Heinz (2002). *Achtung-Panzer! The Development of Tank Warfare.* London: Cassell. Trans. Christopher Duffy; originally published in German in 1937.

Isaev, Aleksey (2010). *Neizvestnyy-1941--Ostanovlennyy-blitskrig* ('The Unknown Blitzkrieg'). Moscow: Penguin. Available online at http://statehistory.ru/books/Aleksey-Isaev_Neizvestnyy-1941--Ostanovlennyy-blitskrig/(accessed 4 February 2014).

Kershaw, Robert (2010). *War without Garlands: Operation Barbarossa 1941–1942.* Weybridge: Ian Allan.

Kirchubel, Robert (2007). *Operation Barbarossa 1941 (3): Army Group Center.* Oxford: Osprey.

Kurowski, Franz (1994). *Infanterie Aces.* Mechanicsburg, PA: Stackpole.

Lemelsen, Joachim & Schmidt, Juliuz (1960). *29. Division, 29. Infanterie Division (mot.).* Bad Nauheim: Podzun-Verlag.

Lucas, James (1991). *War on the Eastern Front, 1941–1945: The German Soldier in Russia.* London: Greenhill.

Lukin, M.F. (1979). 'V Smolenskom srazhenii' ('In the Battle of Smolensk'), in *Voyenno-istoricheskiy zhurnal* ('Military History Journal'), 1979 Vol. 7, pp. 42–45. Available online at rkka.ru/oper/lukin/smol.htm (accessed 4 February 2014).

Macksey, Kenneth (1975). *Guderian, Panzer General.* London: Purnell.

Merridale, Catherine (2005). *Ivan's War: The Red Army 1939–45.* London: Faber & Faber.

Reese, Roger R. (2011). *Why Stalin's Soldiers Fought: The Red Army's Military Effectiveness in World War II.* Lawrence, KA: University Press of Kansas.

Reichswehr (1933). *Truppenführung* ('Troop-leading').

RKKA (1937). *Predvaritel'naya polevoy sluzhby Pravila* ('Provisional Field Regulations').

Rottman, Gordon L. (2007). *Soviet Rifleman 1941–45.* Oxford: Osprey.

Rottman, Gordon L. (2010). *World War II Battlefield Communications.* Oxford: Osprey.

Spaeter, Helmuth (1992). *The History of the Panzerkorps Grossdeutschland Vol. I.* Winnipeg: J.J. Fedorowicz.

Thomas, Nigel (2010). *World War II Soviet Armed Forces (1): 1939–1941.* Oxford: Osprey.

TsAMO (Tsentral'nyy arkhiv Ministerstva oborony Rossiyskoy Federatsii, or 'The Central Archive of the Russian Ministry of Defence'). Available online at http://www.rusarchives.ru (accessed 4 February 2014).

US Army (1942). 'The German Motorized Infantry Regiment'. CARL, Special Series, No. 4.

US Army (1949). 'Peculiarities of Russian Warfare', CARL, German Report Series, MS No. T-22.

Westwood, David (2002). *German Infantryman (1): 1933–40.* Oxford: Osprey.

INDEX

References to illustrations are shown in **bold**.

Boltenstern, Genmaj Walter von 46, **56**
Brodowski, Oblt von 41, 42
Busse, Lt 42

Chernyugov, Col Spyridon S. 31, 34, 35, 38, 40, 43
combat role: German 10–11; Soviet 11–12
communications: German 16–17; Soviet 18–19
Courbière, Oblt de 69–70

Dnieper, River **26**, 30, 31, 43, 46, 48, 51–52
Dremov, Lt-Col Ivan F. 67, 69
dress: German 20–21; Soviet 25

Ehr, Fritz 56
equipment: German 21; Soviet 25
Eremenko, Lt-Gen Andrei I. 58

Fadeyev, Maj Yevgeniy I. 47
Finke, Uffz 51, 52

Gerasimenko, Lt-Gen 75
German Army (Heer)
 Armeekorps (mot.): XXIV. 29, 30, 44; XXXXVI. 59; XXXXVII 46
 'Artillerie Gruppe Broeren'/'Artillerie Gruppe Jauer' 50
 AufklAbt 10: 35, **38**, **39**
 Feldgendarmerie 9
 Heeresgruppe Mitte 30–31, 45, 57, 58
 infantry divisions, motorized 10–11; 10. Infanterie-Division (mot.) 29, 30, 34–35, **38**, 38; 29. Infanterie-Division (mot.) **26**, 46, 47, 50, 50, 51, **52**, 54, 55, 56
 Infanterie-Regiment (mot.) 15: **5**, 46, 48, 50, 51, 52, 53, 54, 73; *Schütze* 20–21
 Infanterie-Regiment (mot.) 20: 23, 30, 44; III./IR 20: 35, 38, 40–41, 42, 43
 Infanterie-Regiment (mot.) 41: **5**, 29, 29–30, 32, 44, 73; I./IR 41 and II./IR 41: 35, **38**, 38, 40–41, 43; III./IR 41: 34, 35, **38**, 38, 40–41, 43
 Infanterie-Regiment (mot.) 71: 46, 50, 51, **52**, 53, 54
 Infanterie-Regiment (mot.) *Großdeutschland* **5**, **11**, **58**, **59**, 59, 62, 63, 63, 67–70, 71; I./IR GD **60**, 60, 62, **66**, 68–70, 71; II./IR GD 62, 63, 67, 70; III./IR GD 62, 67; Leutnant 23
 mortar crew **63**
 motorcycle units (*Kradschützen-Abteilung*) **17**, **39**, 58
 Panzer divisions 10; 3. Panzer-Division 35; 7. Panzer-Division 50; 17. Panzer-Division 55; 18. Panzer-Division 70
 Panzergruppe 2: 29, 31, 45, 76
 Panzergruppe 3: 31, 45
 Pioniere **26**, 46–47, 50–51, 53
 PzJgAbt 10: 23, 30, 35, 42
 PzRgt 6: 30, 40, 41–43, **42**, 44; II./PzRgt 6: 23
 rifle squads (*Schützengruppen*) 19, 22
 SS-Divisions (mot.) 11
Gordov, Maj-Gen Vasily N. 31, 75
Gorodniansky, Maj-Gen Avksentii M. 50, 52, 55
Guderian, Genobst Heinz 10, **16**, 44, 46, 71, 76

Halder, Genobst Franz 56, 73, 77
Hänert, Oblt Karl 62, 71

infantrymen, German **5**, 20–21, **22**, **23**, 46, 76
insignia: German 58; Soviet 15, 25

Jungkunst, Fw Johann 38
Junkers Ju 87 'Stuka' **67**

Kachalov, Lt-Gen Vladimir Y. 18–19, 58–59, 67, 70, 71, 77
Klinter, SS-Hauptsturmführer 13
Komsomol 14
Krylov, Marshal Nikolai I. 14

leadership: German 16–17; Soviet 18, 19
Lemelsen, Gen Joachim 46, **56**
lessons learned: the Germans 72–73; the Soviets 74–75
logistics: German 14; Soviet 16
Löper, Genlt Friedrich-Wilhelm von 44
Luftwaffe 35, 55, **67**, 67, 75
Lukin, Lt-Gen Mikhail F. 47, 47, 53, 55–56

morale: German 13; Soviet 15

Nabokov, Lieutenant 39
Nehring, Genmaj Walther 56
NKVD 14, 15, 58, **77**

officers: German 29, **52**; Soviet **15**, 54
Operation *Barbarossa* 72; central sector, June and July 1941 **6**
origins: German 9–10; Soviet 11

Pavlov, Gen Dmitry G. 15, 77
Petrovsky, Maj-Gen Leonid G. 43, 75
Pobolovo 35, 38
Politruks ('political leaders') 18
Popov, Lieutenant 38–39
prisoners-of-war, Russian 73

railways, Soviet 57 *see also* trains, BP-35 armoured
recruitment: German 12–13; Soviet 14–15
Red Air Force (VVS) 14, **67**
Red Army (RKKA) **11**
 armies: 16th 47, 50, 54, 55–56, 57, 76; 19th and 20th 50, 57; 28th 18–19, 58, 70–71, 76
 artillery **12**
 discipline 15, 77
 Gorodniansky's battle group 50–51, 52, 53, 54
 groups 57–58; Kachalov 58, 70, 71
 Howitzer Artillery Regiment, 707th 31, 34
 infantry **50**, 57, 62
 infantry squad 26, 27
 Light Artillery Regiment, 322nd, 5th Battery **39**
 LMG team 55
 mechanized corps 11
 'RD Fighting Detachment, 117th' 31, 34, 35, **38**, 38, **39**, 40, 44
 reorganizations 11, 12, 47, 77
 Rifle Corps, 34th 54–55
 rifle divisions 11–12; 46th 47, 50, 53, 54; 117th 12, 31, 44; 129th 12, **24**, 47, 50, 53, 54, 55, 54, 76; 145th 12, 58, 62, 63, **66**, 67, 70; 149th 58, 67, 70, 76; 152nd 47
 rifle regiments: 240th 31, **32**, 34, 38, 43, 44, 74; 275th 43; 314th 50–51; 334th 50, 52; 343rd 54; 403rd 70; 457th 24–25, 48, 50, 52, 54, 74; 479th 69; 568th 63, 69; 599th **66**; 729th 66, 67, 69, 74
 Stalin's purges 18, 74, 77
 Tank Division, 57th 47
Reibert, Dr 16
Richthofen, Gen Wolfram von 67
riflemen, Soviet 8, **11**, 24–25, 34, 77
Rössert, Oblt 67, 68

Schütze 20–21 *see also* infantrymen, German
Schwarz, Lt Manfred 42
Seeckt, Genobst Hans von 9–10
sergeant, senior, RKKA **15**
Simon, SS-Gruppenführer Max 73
Smolensk 45, 47, **48**, 48, **52**
Smolensk, battle for 23, 45–47, 50–56, 73, 74; background to battle 45–47; battlefield environment 48; into combat 50–52; 457th Rifle Regiment at 24–25, 48; Infanterie-Regiment (mot.) 15 at 20–21, 48
Spahn, Karl 54
Stalin, Josef **19**, 53; purges 18, 74, 77
Stavka 47, 57, 75

tactics: German 22–23; Soviet 27–28
tanks: German **22**, 23, 42; Soviet **8**, 28
Thomas, Oberst 50
Timoshenko, Marshal Semyon K. **19**, 47, 53
training: German 13, 22; Soviet 26–27
trains, BP-35 armoured 23, 30; Train 16 'Bobruisk' 31, 40, 42
Trotsky, Leon 11
Tukhachevsky, Marshal Mikhail N. 18, 74, 77

Vas'kovo **60**, 66
Vas'kovo–Voroshilovo, battle of 18–19, 57–59, 62–63, 67–71, 73, 74; background to battle 57–59; battlefield environment **60**; clash at Vas'kovo 66; into combat 62–63, 67; Infanterie-Regiment (mot.) *Großdeutschland* at **60**; 729th Rifle Regiment at 60
vehicles, German: motorcycles **5**, **17**, **39**; SdKfz 10/4 half-track **5**, 51; SdKfz 222 armoured car 35, 35; SdKfz 231 armoured car 13; SdKfz 232 armoured car 35; SdKfz 250 half-track **59**; SdKfz 251 APCs 19, 22; StuG assault gun **68**; trucks 9, 19, 22; *see also* tanks: German
vehicles, Soviet 16 *see also* tanks: Soviet
Volkhin, Maj-Gen Alexander 63, 67, 68
Voroshilovo, battle of *see* Vas'kovo–Voroshilovo, battle of

weapons, German 19; anti-aircraft guns 31, 51; anti-tank guns 13, **41**; anti-tank rifles 75; assault gun, StuG **68**; grenades 21; howitzer, 10.5cm leFH 18 light **8**; machine gun, MG 34 light 19, **22**, 66; mortars **63**; rifle, Mauser Kar 98k 21
weapons, Soviet 26; anti-tank gun, 45mm 40; bayonets 25; grenades 70; gun, 76mm divisional **11**; howitzer-gun, 152mm **12**; machine guns 26, **28**, 54, 55; mortars 11, 27; revolver, Nagant 18, 38; rifle, Mosin-Nagant **25**, 26, 38; rifle, SVT-40 26, 38; rifles, anti-tank 75
Wedel, Lt von 42

Zakharov, Maj-Gen 69
Zeider, Schütze Benno 12–13
Zhlobin **32**, 32
Zhlobin, battle of 23, 29–31, **32**, 34–35, 38–44, 73, 74–75; background to battle 29–31; battlefield environment 32, 34; into combat 34–35; Infanterie-Regiment (mot.) 41 at 32; RKKA surrounded at Pobolovo 35, 38, 38; 240th Rifle Regiment at **32**
Zhukov, Gen Georgy K. 57, 58
Zobel, Lt Horst **17**, 35